JR VERSUS STINKY DUMPING GROUND

R. ELLIS BROWN

JR Versus Stinky Dumping Ground

Copyright © 2026 by R. Ellis Brown

Paperback ISBN: 979-8-9940831-0-9
Hardcover: 979-8-9940831-1-6

Editor: The Publishing Pad

Cover Designer: Peter Ogundipe

TABLE OF CONTENTS

CHAPTER 1

I'M GOING TO ENJOY RULING THE WORLD.

But right now, I lie in bed thinking of the burial. It has been about two weeks since my little sister's funeral, and I'm having trouble sleeping again. After trying, like, forever to go to sleep, I give up and decide to daydream the night away. But that does not work either, so I head down the stairs to the kitchen. *Some food should make me sleepy.*

My parents have beat me to the refrigerator. They are getting a late-night snack, most likely the leftover jerk chicken. This is very unfair. They do not let me eat late at night, but here they are tearing through the fridge looking for food.

I murmur to myself, "Okay, I will double back when they are done." If there is anything I have learned from my twelve years on this earth, it is that catching an adult being unfair will not change their decision. As I turn to head back upstairs, I realize that Mom and Dad are talking about me, the way adults talk about kids behind our backs.

Between chews, Mom says, "I'm worried about JR. He is always so anxious. I hope he's not too stressed out."

My name is Jamal Reynolds, but everyone calls me JR.

My dad munches as he talks. "If he is stressed, he's hiding it well…eating everything in sight."

"But not an ounce of emotion during the funeral. No tears," my mom says sadly.

There is silence. I feel bad that they are worrying about me. They have enough on their minds.

I shake my head and think, *I'm okay. I feel great. Never been better.*

In the kitchen, my mom continues, "He hasn't been debating when we tell him to do something."

They both chuckle. I don't see anything that is funny.

Dad adds, "No snarkiness, no arguing over everything."

Of course not! This has been a stressful time for them, so I have been trying really, really hard not to upset them. For example, I have not been pointing out their flaws and mistakes.

Now is definitely not a good time to eat, so I continue heading back toward my room. I will find a way to survive without food until breakfast.

Then I hear the ominous words from Mom. "Maybe he is acting up at other places, like school. We should keep in touch with his school."

Dad ends with, "Yep, he is sure to take advantage of their sympathy."

* * *

I hear my parents go back to their bedroom. I finally give up on trying to sleep, get up, and look out the window of my bedroom. Looking over the rooftops of my neighborhood, I can make out some lights of skyscrapers in downtown Manhattan. The lights of Manhattan always seem to be calling you to come closer. Not me, however. I am happy right where I am in Brooklyn.

Suddenly there is some movement near the locked gate of the empty lot next to my house. Despite the ten-foot metal fencing surrounding Stinky Dump—that is what I call the empty lot—I can still see some parts of it.

I open the window of my second-floor room and hear the faint sound of a truck engine idling. Then it shifts into gear, and soon a garbage truck backs up to the gate, which is right at the corner where my street begins. Someone gets out of the garbage truck, unlocks the gate, and then gets back in. The garbage truck reverses into Stinky Dump. It stops in an area of Stinky Dump that is not visible to me because it is blocked by the ten-foot fence. This has been happening a few times a week for the last year or so.

I was really, really curious about what was happening over there in Stinky Dump. There are so many dangers out there.

I shiver a little and bite my nails at the thought of something happening to my family. I do not want to lose another family member. Plus, I cannot sleep. There is only one thing I can do to keep my family safe: investigate this myself! With everything that has been going on, I know I am unlikely to be punished if I'm caught.

I rub my hands together in excitement at the promise of adventure. I put on some jeans, a sweatshirt, and an older pair of sneakers, thinking, *this should be enough to keep me warm in the early spring weather.* I grab my phone and tiptoe down the stairs. The neighborhood is fairly safe, so my parents have never installed a burglar alarm. I slowly, carefully open the front door, step outside, and close the door just as carefully. I go down the steps and lift the gate as I open it. That is the way to avoid any squeaks.

I turn left and make my way toward Stinky Dump. I stay close to the wall, as that is what soldiers do when they are on patrol.

I peek through the open gate of Stinky Dump. The garbage truck's engine is idling, and the grill is facing me. I hear some activity going on behind the truck. I unlock my phone and take photos of the truck and its license plate.

This is going really smoothly. I did not know patrolling could be so much fun. I'm curious about what the driver is dumping. I quietly move into the empty lot and walk past the truck. *Ah, the driver is digging a hole.* His back is to the truck and me. I look into the garbage truck and see a bunch of garbage in red bags.

I take some pictures of the red bags. Then I reach for one, thinking I have time to open it to see what is inside. That is when I hear the voice of someone approaching through the gate of Stinky Dump . . . the voice of the driver's assistant, apparently.

The assistant is grumbling, "Okay, I got the BLT sandwiches and the beers. I swear, the next time the bodega guy messes up my order, I'm gonna smack him."

The approaching assistant sounds like a roughneck, which is what we call rowdy people. *I have to get out of here!* It sounds like he is coming around the truck from the right-hand side, the same way I did. I head around to the truck's left side to hide behind the truck and avoid him.

As I make my way around the back of the truck, I look down into the hole. It is a fairly deep hole that cannot be seen from any house. The driver is down inside the hole, making it deeper with a shovel.

I have a flashback to my little sister Joan's grave. This hole looks similar, just broader.

It looks like they plan to bury some red bags in the hole.

Just as I am looking down into the hole, the driver looks up in the direction of the voice of his assistant. He must be eager for the approaching food. Of course, when he looks up, he sees me looking down at him. We stare at each other for a second. Both of us are surprised.

I panic and run as the driver yells out, "Grab him! This is private property. Thief! Did you steal something?"

I cannot imagine why he would think I was a thief. There is nothing of value in a dumping ground.

I run around past the left side of the truck and right into the assistant, who was not as far into Stinky Dump as I originally thought. We both fall. The BLT sandwiches burst open, and lettuce flies everywhere.

I am younger and more fit, so I am back on my feet first. I run toward the gate of Stinky Dump, but the assistant manages to grab my leg.

"That's my dinner you messed with," snarls the assistant as he grabs my pant leg. I kick and try to free myself from his grasp. One of my kicks lands on his face, as he is still lying on the ground while holding on to my leg. I hear a sound of pain and a common curse word coming from the assistant.

But now I hear the driver approaching also, so there will soon be two of them.

My first panicked thought is that I cannot allow my family to go through another tragedy. How would they ever get through losing yet another child?

At this point, what I plan to do is wriggle away and go into my fighting stance, facing the two men. They will come at me, and I'll deliver a back kick that sends one of them flying. I will then effortlessly deliver a side kick to the jaw of the approaching second man, and while they lie unconscious, I will . . .

. . . Okay, okay. Seriously, now. After I wriggle away, I run for dear life—like I have never run before—through the gate of Stinky Dump and onto the street. However, they catch me again when I stumble and fall, and the driver throws a punch that lands squarely on the back of my shoulder.

It hurts. I scream in pain, and it startles them for a moment. I do manage to kick the driver in the shin before I take off again.

I hear curses coming from behind me, something about a homeless kid whom no one will miss when they catch him. They are running after me again when an arm reaches out and grabs me.

CHAPTER 2

"JR, WHAT'RE YOU DOING OUT HERE THIS time of night?" It is Auntie Mabel, my neighbor, walking her dog. She lives alone and is always out and about at the strangest of times.

She calls out to the men, "I saw you hit him!" She is not at all scared.

The two thugs stop when they see Auntie Mabel.

"I said you better leave this boy alone if you know what's good for you."

Rusty, Auntie Mabel's pit bull, growls at them. I am surprised, as in all the years I have known him, Rusty has never made a sound. He usually walks with his head down as if he is ashamed of something he did. He is so timid that even Joan, my sister who recently died, would pet him, and Joan was very scared of big dogs.

"Don't you know the boy is still mourning?" says Auntie Mabel as she pulls me close and wraps her arm around my shoulders.

I rub the back of my shoulder where I was hit and stay close to Auntie Mabel.

The driver is infuriated. "That little thief stole my phone," he says, and he points at my phone that I am still holding. I don't know what he is talking about, but he continues. "He snuck into the cab of my truck and stole—"

"That's a lie." Surrounded by Auntie Mabel and Rusty, I feel brave enough to express my opinion. "Both of you are simpletons."

My grandpa would have called the driver and his assistant "simpletons." It was his favorite word, and I think it applies to many people in my life.

The driver squints at the phone I'm holding in my hand. "Oh, that's not my phone. I thought you had taken my phone."

"Well, then. You owe him an apology," says Auntie Mabel.

The driver and his assistant look at Rusty the pit bull and make a tactical decision to retreat. As they disappear into Stinky Dump, the driver retorts, "I just caught him before he stole something. Why is he sneaking around a locked, empty lot in the middle of the night, anyway?"

The driver and his assistant do not do any more digging. Instead, they whisper between themselves for a few seconds. Then the driver hops into the truck and drives it into the street. The assistant quickly locks the gate and gets into the truck, and they drive away.

Auntie Mabel shakes her head and asks me, "What the hell are they up to?"

Before I can answer, Auntie Mabel, her hand still on my shoulder, turns me around and pulls me along with her. "Come with me. I made some pound cake today. Let's stop by my house before I take you home."

I agree with Auntie Mabel that we should eat something, as it is my duty to keep the lonely neighbor company. Also, it will give me time to talk her out of snitching to my parents and getting me in trouble.

I enter her house with great anticipation, and Auntie Mabel puts me to sit at her kitchen table. Rusty lazily walks to a cushion in the corner and sits on it. Auntie Mabel pulls out half of a yellow pound cake with lemon icing while saying, "Would you like ice cream with this? Is chocolate ice cream okay?"

I nod in approval and try to be sociable. "Who already ate half of your pound cake, Auntie Mabel?"

"Oh, I had some of it this morning. And I always give some to the mailman and those other poor drivers who are making deliveries, like Mr. Polk. Plus, anyone who is unlucky enough to make the mistake of engaging me in conversation."

We both laugh heartily as I dig into a generous slice of pound cake and anxiously await the chocolate ice cream.

"Do you ever get lonely living here by yourself, Auntie Mabel?" I am practicing the art of conversation. It seems to better position you to get what you want from adults.

"Sometimes! I can't wait for my son to get back from the Army," Auntie Mabel says as she places a hunk of chocolate ice cream beside the pound cake. "As a matter of fact, you remind me of my son."

"Oh, how is he doing?"

"He's coming back the week after next Friday," says Auntie Mabel as she sits and rubs her hands with glee.

I look around at the photographs of her only son, the soldier. He was a cool guy, but he did not seem to spend much time at Auntie Mabel's even when he was home on leave. Being mature, I do not pry.

"Now, young man, tell me what you were doing out at night being chased by a pair of hooligans."

"Well, Auntie Mabel, I could not sleep, so I investigated those guys in Stinky Dump. They could be dumping nuclear waste. Ms. Bridges from our school library is putting together an exhibit on nuclear waste. She said when nuclear bombs are made, they produce a lot of nuclear waste, like nuclear garbage you must throw out."

"Stinky Dump? Is that what you call that eyesore of an empty lot?" Auntie Mabel chuckles. "Haha. I love it. Great name! You young people and your imaginations. And those two guys who were chasing you, they wouldn't know nuclear waste if it blew up in their faces."

"Really!"

"They clearly aren't the brightest of bulbs. They must work for someone who owns the lot. Probably some big-shot developer."

I remark, "Ah, so the simpletons work for the owner, huh, Auntie Mabel?"

Auntie Mabel ignores my question. "Now look, JR, I think I have to tell your parents about tonight."

"Mom and Dad have been through a lot recently. I don't want to stress them out any more."

Auntie Mabel hesitates. Apparently, as an adult, she is required to snitch. I must act quickly.

"I promise not to go back to Stinky Dump if you do not tell them," I plead.

Auntie Mabel hesitates again. My face is surely covered with chocolate ice cream sprinkled with crumbs of pound cake. I hope it adds to my sad, adorable look.

Auntie Mabel is still flustered. "Okay, uhm, let me think about it. What you did was very dangerous."

I think the episode is over. Little did I know how her words will come back to haunt me.

After I talk Auntie Mabel out of walking me home, I sneak back into my house and quietly climb the stairs to my bedroom.

What are the guys in Stinky Dump hiding?

CHAPTER 3

UH-OH . . . MS. ALLIE IS TALKING TO ME. I have been daydreaming in her Social Studies class again, but not the usual daydreams about what I will do to fix the world when I'm in charge. Today, thoughts of Joan keep entering my mind.

I think Ms. Allie asked me a question just before I came out of my daydream, but now I'm struggling to remember it.

I wrack my brain. At this stage it is too late to remember the exact question, but if I could recall what she has been talking about, maybe I can guess the question and then give her the answer.

When my mind left the class and entered the world of my daydreams, Ms. Allie had been droning on and on and on and on. "Brooklyn is one of the five boroughs of New York City . . ."

Then she said something about the people. "The first inhabitants were the American Indians . . ."

I think I went into my daydream when she said, ". . . extensive mosaic of ethnicities to be found today . . ."

I like Ms. Allie and her energy. She came to New York City right after graduating from college, became a teacher, and was still excited by everything. She made me feel like I was lucky to be living in New York City.

I am a student at the Breukelen Middle School (BMS) on the border of Bushwick and Bedford-Stuyvesant in Brooklyn. The school recently evolved into one of those institutions where everyone has a hands-on approach to helping us kids. Generally, the parents and teachers are a little too energetic in this regard for my taste. I know of some schools where no one, parent or teacher, seems to care about the kids. At BMS, the teachers are always up in your business. Anyway, I do not complain, as I know that the alternative is worse.

"Do you know the answer, JR?" repeated Ms. Allie.

Oh, so I *have* been asked a question. I know if I ask Ms. Allie to repeat it, she will refuse.

I think hard. *If Ms. Allie has been talking about Brooklyn, then the answer must be . . .*

"Brooklyn!" I shout confidently.

"No, JR. The capital of the USA is Washington, DC."

Okay, she got me that time.

"We finished talking about Brooklyn quite a while ago," Ms. Allie adds as the simpletons in my class laugh.

That last remark was not needed, coming as it did in addition to the scolding. I had already taken the loss, so there was no reason for her to dwell on it. Ms. Allie is spiking the ball after scoring. It's an over-the-top celebration on her part, and she would be penalized in any sporting situation.

Now I am going to get it. She will start scolding me and could possibly escalate the confrontation to the point of confining me against my will, perhaps in detention. I can tell that Ms. Allie is about to launch her offensive.

"Sorry, Ms. Allie," I say. "I guess I have a lot on my mind."

Ms. Allie approaches my desk, pauses, and looks at me sadly. "Look, JR, try to pay attention, okay? We'll be discussing the semester project next, and you have to find a topic." She rubs my shoulder, then smiles at me and turns away.

I exhale. It looks like I will be avoiding trouble of any sort. The other kids also look surprised and sad, seeing as how they will not get the pleasure of seeing a fellow classmate tortured and burned at the stake. *Simpletons.*

My daydreams are very important. Daydreaming is fun and easy, and nobody gets hurt. I plan to rule the world by the time I am twenty. Many of my daydreams involve planning how I will become ruler of the world and what I will do—in addition to taking care of Mom and Dad—to make the world better for myself . . . and for everyone else, also.

Ms. Allie goes back to teaching social studies, so I try to go back to daydreaming. No luck! I was a good daydreamer before Joan died.

Ms. Allie talks about the class project. "Your project should be about something you think is important. Do a project about something that is bothering you."

CHAPTER 4

I ENJOY MY WALKS HOME FROM SCHOOL with my two friends, Roberto and Maya. It's the highlight of my day. The highlight of my entire life, really.

I enjoy these brief times of freedom with Roberto and Maya. Due to a school initiative to raise more independent kids, our parents recently started letting us walk the six blocks to and from school without adults monitoring and snooping on us. It seems the school got all the neighborhood businesses and the rest of the community to keep an eye out for anyone trying to do us harm. Also, I think they want the community to snitch on us if they catch us doing anything wrong. Anyway, this new program is cool! It's much cooler than having to wait around for someone to pick me up after school.

As we approach Stinky Dump, I lag behind Roberto and Maya. "Have I been walking more slowly since Joan died?" I ask my two friends.

"Yes" comes the reply from both.

I remember how I would pick up Joan at her school and she would walk home with us. She would walk either too slowly or too fast instead of keeping pace with us.

"You've also been forgetting stuff we tell you," says Roberto.

"Look," I reply. "I'm fine. I'm good. Never been better."

"And you haven't been concentrating in class," adds Maya.

Roberto now says, "That was pretty slick, JR, the way you finessed Ms. Allie to get off from being punished."

"It was just my normal sad face," I reply. "It's worked in the past."

Maya disagrees. "No, it has not worked in the past. And it was not your normal sad face."

Roberto nods in agreement with Maya.

"Do you think people are treating me differently? Like, have I been getting away with stuff?"

They continue to nod.

"I hope some of it rubs off on us," says Maya. "People think of us as a team."

"Yep, I could use some of that," adds Roberto.

I stop in front of Stinky Dump. Roberto and Maya take a few more steps before they realize I am not with them. They stop and look back at me, staring through a gap between the fence and the gate.

Roberto says, "Don't go in there again. You may not be as lucky this time."

All three of us laugh. Earlier today, I told them about my adventure last night in Stinky Dump. I tried to make myself look braver, but I don't think they believed me.

"So many bad things happen in Stinky Dump," I tell them. "My dad says the real owner must be a powerful person who does not have to follow the rules."

Roberto and Maya agree.

Maya says, "Yeah. Remember when I was walking by here with your big sister, Ayesha, and a drug addict grabbed her and tried to pull her inside? We screamed so loudly the whole neighborhood came out to see what was wrong. I got a chance to call 911." Maya wants to be a detective when she becomes an adult.

I describe another event. "Remember, like, five years ago when my big brother disobeyed Mom and Dad's direct orders and climbed the fence to play there?"

"Yeah!" remarks Roberto. "And he fell into an uncovered hole and fractured his leg."

By now, both Roberto and Maya are standing beside me and looking into Stinky Dump.

Roberto recalls more of the event. "I remember the ambulance arriving and the firefighters cutting the lock on the fence to get to him."

"He still hasn't been punished for that," I remark.

We all shake our heads in disbelief.

I continue my rant. "I was on Dad's side on that one. I thought Junior should have been punished to the max, considering he disobeyed his own parents. Ayesha agreed with us. But then Mom had some unrelated comment about how the pain of the fracture was enough punishment."

"So unfair!" . . . "Not right!" say my two friends in support.

Roberto ends with, "My dad says Stinky Dump brings down property values." Roberto is always into the numbers.

I look at the overgrown grass behind the locked gate. Stinky Dump is triggering to my family. Nothing good ever happens over there.

After a while, Roberto and Maya pull me away.

As we walk away, I declare, "So you guys think people have been treating me differently, huh? I will check on it right now and let you know."

CHAPTER 5

I VISIT OUR FRIDGE AS SOON AS I'm home. I'm leaning into the open door when the sound of approaching footsteps startles me. Should I call 911? Is this going to be another dangerous situation like last night at Stinky Dump?

I know if I yell loudly enough, Auntie Mabel may hear. This situation is serious. *An uninvited guest in my house! Where should I hide?*

I am about to run for it when I realize it is just my dad getting ready for a subway shift. I let out a sigh of relief. Since Joan's burial, every little thing has made me uneasy. I have to keep this to myself, as the others are still stressed, and I have to take care of them.

My dad appears in the doorway, and I suddenly feel more at ease. To this day, I still remember in second grade when we had parents come to the class to talk about their jobs. My dad showed up in his MTA uniform with a lot of keys attached to his belt. My dad's job is one of my major claims to fame, and I bring it up whenever possible. A girl even asked me, "How do you get a dad? They seem cool to have."

I claimed that my dad sometimes let me drive the subway train, and I began making much progress in the class status rankings—until Tyrone and Keyshia called me on it. I hate them. Simpletons!

I go back to poking around in the refrigerator. Normally, Dad would have some snarky remark about how much food his kids eat. However, this time, he picks me up and throws me over his shoulder. He has not done this recently. It was the type of thing he would often do to Joan when she was alive. I scream happily, as I enjoy it, but I feel I am getting too big to indulge in this type of behavior in public. I make a mental note to warn Dad not to do it when my friends are around.

"How are things going, little JR?"

And that is my first warning that I am on the way to being the new baby of the family. You see, my dad usually just calls me JR. Not Baby JR or Little JR or any of that weird stuff. Even though I am the most mature person in the entire house, my dad needs to have a baby in the family, and it looks like he wants it to be me.

So my parents are treating me differently!

After filling my stomach with some red velvet cake I find in the kitchen, I go upstairs to my room. I now have the bedroom to myself because my brother, Junior, moved into the basement after our tenant finally left. My dad had breathed a sigh of relief because the tenant had not paid rent for many months. She finally decided to leave the city, as she claimed it was becoming a hellhole. That is how we were finally able to get rid of her.

I hear my dad leaving for work at the same time I hear my older sister, Ayesha, returning home. She enters her room next to mine and locks the door.

I am about to daydream again, but I change my mind. It has become difficult to concentrate since Joan died.

My sister Ayesha is the only other person in the house, so I decide to keep her company whether she wants me to or not. She never allows me into her room, but I will be able to annoy her from outside. I can also check if she is going to treat me differently.

I go to Ayesha's door and knock gently. I plan to increase the intensity of the knocks until she grows annoyed and yells, "Stop it!" and "Go away, Germ."

About five seconds later, when I am about to start a second round of more intensive knocking, the door opens, and I wait for her to start yelling.

Instead of being told to get lost, I get a smile and some nice words. "JR! I forgot you were home. What're you doing?"

Her niceness catches me off guard, and I whisper, "Nothing."

Ayesha smiles at me, then reaches out and grabs my wrist. "Come on in!"

I am suspicious and wonder if I should run away, but I am already in her room. Ayesha pulls me over to her desk, sits in the chair, and gestures for me to sit on the bed next to her chair. She goes back to her phone, which is lying on the desk, and talks into it. "JR is here. I am taking care of him today."

Oh, really! Ayesha is a high school sophomore and, in my opinion, lacks maturity among many other things. The only thing Ayesha is good for is making brownies. Yes, I must admit she makes really good brownies and shares them generously.

I am about to say something nasty when the voices of a gaggle of girls come at me through the speaker of Ayesha's smartphone.

The friends—I believe there are four of them, but it could be five—all enthusiastically greet me at the same time. "Hi, JR." . . . "Kisses, JR!" . . . "How're you doing?" I instinctively lean back in surprise. Normally they are never nice because their minds have been poisoned by the things Ayesha tells them about me.

Ayesha continues. "I'm babysitting my baby brother. So yeah!"

"That is so nice of you, helping your baby brother get through this rough time."

My sister usually refers to me as Germ, not baby brother. Ayesha smiles over at me as if I'm supposed to be impressed at her giggling group of friends. So immature. *Such simpletons.*

I am about to let everyone know that I do not need to be babysat, especially by someone who is less mature than I am. However, before I can utter a word, the girls ignore me and go back to discussing whatever they were discussing before I was dragged into Ayesha's room.

They are all trying to talk at the same time, and I cannot follow because there are several topics being discussed, with references to topics that were previously discussed and other references to topics they plan to discuss soon.

As a matter of fact, for a good ten seconds, each of the five of them—or is it six?—are speaking at the same time about five—or six—different topics.

"... I hate her. What was that thing she was wearing today?"

"... That is sure to show up on the next quiz. Deadass!"

"... and no one even invited her to sit at our lunch table."

"... I may let him kiss me just to keep him around until better comes along ..."

"... and Coach was trying to kick me off the dance team, when I'm the only one who can groove ..."

"... I really hate her. Those outfits she wears to school are tragic." I think that might be the same girl I heard first. Or not. I dunno.

I quietly get up to leave the room. I would rather be daydreaming. Ayesha looks over at me. "Aren't you going to keep me company?" Ayesha shared her room with Joan before Joan died, so I gather I am supposed to be the replacement when she is lonely.

I'm a little torn, but she has four or five friends on the phone. How can she be lonely? "I have some things to do," I whisper.

As is her usual way, Ayesha issues an order. "Stay a little while." She then turns back to the phone and her cackling friends, ignoring me completely.

I feel guilty leaving Ayesha alone, but I sneak out, and she does not even notice. As I leave, I take a quick look back at her talking nonsense on the phone. Joan's things were removed from the room right after her burial. I guess my parents thought it would help Ayesha to heal. I wish I had kept some of Joan's favorite toys. They were donated to needy kids, so that felt cool.

Anyway . . . *Ayesha treats me differently!*

On my way to my room, I am curious if my big brother Junior is at home yet. I head down the stairs to the basement.

Ah, my brother is there. Junior is useful when it comes to playing sports with me. Otherwise, I could tell you a long list of his faults.

Junior is a graduating high school senior and has turned the basement into his own man cave since being allowed to take it over. In the basement with my brother is his friend Malcolm. I approve of Malcolm. Malcolm usually speaks to me like I'm an adult. I remember how at Joan's funeral, he realized how sad I was and sat next to me to perk me up.

Malcolm said to me, "I can tell you are sad, but you are not even crying?"

I looked up at him, pouted, and shrugged.

"It's okay to cry."

"I don't feel like crying," I reply.

"Okay! Your family may need you more than you think, so look out for them."

He must have meant that my family needed me to be their new baby.

Right now, Junior and Malcolm are fixing an electric bike in the basement and don't even acknowledge my presence as I enter. Malcolm is an expert at fixing anything with mechanical issues. While rehabbing the bike, they are complaining about the performance of the New York Knicks basketball team.

I see that they have some Krazy Glue. They stop me from playing with it when I try to touch it.

While I approve of Malcolm, my mom thinks he is a bad influence. Malcolm had a very hard-luck upbringing, including a broken family and time in foster homes. He barely made it through high school and was the only member of his family to have gotten even that far in the quest to be educated. Malcolm is not planning on going to college, but he wants to learn a trade and use his mechanical skills. Meanwhile, Junior was recently accepted to Howard University and is looking forward to starting there in the fall.

Junior and Malcolm pack up and get ready to leave.

"Where are you going?" I pry.

There is hesitation. Then they answer that they are going to the neighborhood park to meet friends.

I put on my sad face, and Junior goes, "Do you wanna come with us?"

Malcolm insists, "Yeah, come hang with us. Meet some fly babes."

Junior's eyes light up as he tells Malcolm, "You know, if I tell them I'm babysitting my baby brother to cheer him up, that should work."

There is that word *baby* again!

Malcolm nods. "That is so true."

They fist-bump each other. I do an eye roll, and Malcolm puts his arm around my shoulders.

"Nah, c'mon. We really want you to hang with us."

In the past, my brother would not have taken me along. But now, he also insists. "Yeah, you'll enjoy it. It will be fun for you," he says sincerely.

So my brother treats me differently!

I think it's worth a try to press my luck. "Maybe I can ride the electric bike. It's a long way to the park."

They laugh uproariously. "You are too much," says Malcolm as he grabs the bike.

"You walk more to get to school. I can't with you," chuckles Junior.

So I get to ride the electric bike alongside them as we go to the park. *Just because Junior is about to graduate and go to college, he sure has gotten a lot of freedom to do whatever the hell he wants*, I think as we head toward the park.

I'm looking forward to hanging out with more mature women than my sister's friends. "What are we going to do at the park?"

I'm ignored as Junior and Malcolm talk between themselves.

I do not give up. "Are we going to jump the subway turnstiles? Hey, do you guys plan to roof-surf on the subway cars?"

This gets their attention. My brother looks at me with raised eyebrows. "Are you crazy?"

Malcolm joins in. "Subway surfing is dangerous. Don't you ever do that!"

"Well, my dad says that it is dangerous, but some teenagers still do it," I reply.

My brother plays like he is pushing me off the e-bike. "We're going to hang out. Just chill and enjoy."

We arrive at the park, and I am disappointed to find out that the dozen or so seniors from my brother's school are not planning to do anything cool. What is the use of having all this freedom if you don't use it properly?

Instead, they sit around talking about colleges and what majors and careers they plan to pursue. I thought that at least the girls would be more interesting. But they don't seem to be interested in me as a person. Rather, they see me as an object—a baby. Junior's friends speak to me like I'm a child and don't take me seriously. They stroke my head (girls) or pat me on the shoulder (guys) and ask me if I miss my little sister. *Of course I do. Wouldn't you, you simpleton?* However, the women do smell good with their perfumes, so I held back from making my true thoughts known. I can be very diplomatic when I need to be.

The only useful part of this boring event is being fed with a beef patty. Apparently there is some booze hidden somewhere, because a slightly drunk Malcolm grabs me and stares into my eyes.

After staring at me for a while, he says, "I been watching your family because I have always liked the way you guys operate as a unit. You are very lucky. I wish I'd had that when I was coming up. That is one reason I stay close."

Oops. I hope he does not find out that my mom is suspicious of him. Mom does not like anyone who hangs around her family.

Malcolm continues, "Lemme tell you something. Everyone in your family is sad even though they try not to show it. You must think about them and help them get their groove back. You may be the baby now, but babies have responsibilities also."

What responsibilities could a baby have? They just eat, sleep, cry, and poop.

But the beef patty is good. If you balance it out, being considered the baby has some downsides, but it seems like it might still be a pretty good deal for me. I can try to cut Roberto and Maya in on the deal.

Little did I know that the value of being the family baby and teachers' pet would change that very night. The disadvantages would rear their head.

Babies are never taken seriously.

CHAPTER 6

LATER THAT EVENING, I'M SITTING IN MY bedroom and look out at Stinky Dump, my chin resting on my hands. I had been planning to daydream about some of the things I will do when I rule the world, but thoughts of Joan and the many times we rushed her to the emergency room keep crossing my mind. The more I look at Stinky Dump, the more dangerous it looks, and the more it seems like the culprit.

There is a knock on my door, and Mom and Dad immediately enter. They catch me sitting and looking out the window, head resting on my hands. I did not bother to move from this position when I heard the knock.

I turn around to look at them and find helpless looks on their faces. I suddenly realize that seeing their child looking sadly out the window soon after burying his sister must be disturbing to them. I immediately force a smile onto my face to reassure them. They are very fragile right now with the recent loss of Joan.

"Are you okay, JR?" asks Mom.

"Why didn't you answer the door?" adds Dad.

"You didn't give me a chance to answer the door before bursting in," I reply.

"Well, that answer sounds like the old JR," says Dad. An ever-so-slight smile crosses his face as my mom rolls her eyes.

They sit on the side of my bed without asking permission. *Oh no! They want to talk. What is the problem now?* Mom and Dad stare at me, and I stare back at them over my shoulder.

"Turn around. Talk to us," says Mom as Dad does a circular motion with his hands.

I try not to sigh. I turn around and look at them with the most cheerful look I can muster.

Mom kicks off with, "Ms. Allie says you have not been paying attention in class."

"She is worried about leaving you alone," says Dad.

Wow! Do adults have a hotline to snitch on kids? This just happened today, and Ms. Allie could not even wait a day or two to snitch.

"Also, Auntie Mabel says she caught you wandering around the empty lot next door," says Mom.

I am appalled. But at least Auntie Mabel waited a whole day to snitch, if that is any comfort.

"We're worried about you, son. Why would you sneak out and go into that empty lot?"

I reply confidently, "I wanted to double-check the security around the house."

They do not believe me. Dad continues, "Auntie Mabel says you were chased by two thugs who were trying to hurt you."

"But they didn't," I point out.

My reply is ignored as Mom cries out with a lot of emotion: "You could have been killed! We don't want to lose another child!"

This is getting deep. Those were my exact thoughts when I was being chased by the Stinky Dump simpletons. I do not have a ready answer and just stare at my mom and dad blankly.

"You are so distracted and not your normal self. We think this may not be the time to let you do more things on your own," says my dad. "We agree with Ms. Allie."

I stutter. "W-what do you mean?"

"Well . . ." Mom puts her arm around me and pulls me close.

This is trouble. Worse than getting yelled at.

"We don't want you to be alone," Mom continues, "so we are arranging to have you picked up after school by Auntie Mabel."

"What?" I shout. "Every other kid in school has the freedom to get home by themselves! I'll be the laughingstock of the school."

"It's only until you get . . . until things get back to normal," Dad says.

"I'm not a baby!"

"Sure. When you can show that you are more focused, we will stop treating you like a kid." Dad forces a smile and nods at me as he says this.

"Roberto and Maya can keep me company. They've got my back."

"They're kids also. Maybe they can walk with you and Auntie Mabel," says Mom.

"It will only be for a short time," adds Dad.

"Also, would you like to move into Junior's room in the basement so you can be with him? You had so much fun when you shared this room together." Mom smiles as she sweeps her hand around my room.

No, I did not have fun sharing my room with that simpleton! "Look, I am fine. I am good. Never been better."

Dad tries to explain. "Your actions last night show that you need a little structure. Plus, we really don't want anything bad to happen to you."

An adult picking me up at school while other kids can stroll down the street without a care in the world? I am not a baby. This is a total loss of my freedom. It sounds unconstitutional.

I blame Stinky Dump for ruining my life. I must do something to stop this nonsense.

CHAPTER 7

I EXPLAIN THE SITUATION TO ROBERTO AND Maya as we walk to school next morning. This may be my last walk of freedom.

"But doesn't she pick up those kindergarten kids also?" asks Maya.

"Yeah, so you will be walking home with a bunch of noisy kindergarteners," concludes Roberto.

This cannot be happening to me. Roberto and Maya are sympathetic, but I need more than that.

We run into Mr. Polk, one of the delivery workers who covers our area. We wish him a good morning.

"Gotta go," he says. "I'm running behind. Not gonna be back here until late, late, late this afternoon." Mr. Polk is always running late. He is already in his vehicle and driving away by the time he has finished talking.

Farther down the road, we run into Auntie Mabel looking in the direction of Mr. Polk driving away. She smiles at the three of us, then at me. "I'll be waiting outside your school for you this afternoon, JR. Is that Mr. Polk driving away? He is supposed to have a package for me from my son. I have to sign for it."

I think quickly. "Oh—he said he will be back in the early to mid-afternoon with his final deliveries. You can catch him then."

"Oh, no! But I must pick you up from school."

I reply confidently, "That's okay! Roberto and Maya will take care of me."

"Oh, good!" says Auntie Mabel.

The whole conversation occurred without me missing a stride. It must have seemed like no big deal to Auntie Mabel. After we walk a few steps, Roberto and Maya look at me with admiration.

"Wow! Well done. Very smooth! I'm impressed," they recite together.

* * *

I corner Ms. Allie after class. Like all teachers, she is always in a hurry, but I know she will stop to talk to me. I am sure the teachers have discussed among themselves that I should be treated gently. I may as well take advantage of this while it is available.

The first words from her mouth are, "I hear your parents have someone picking you up from school."

I swear, adults talk too much.

She tells me this while doing a half-kneel. I learned that adults do this kneeling trick so they can lure kids into feeling comfortable by being at their eye level. Then, when you relax, they can more easily pounce and sucker-punch you, usually by pointing out something you did wrong.

However, I have been growing taller, so the adults no longer kneel all the way. Instead, they do a half-kneel.

"I already have Roberto and Maya to ride with me," I respond.

"Oh, but your parents are concerned. They don't want you to get hurt." Then Ms. Allie remembers that I am the one who came to talk to her. "What did you want to talk about?"

"Well, I want to do my project on Stinky Dump. You said we should do our projects on something we think is important."

"What is Stinky Dump?"

I explain the history of Stinky Dump and why I call it that. I was going to include the part it played in the death of Joan, but I decide not to at this time. I do include Roberto and Maya.

"Oh, are Roberto and Maya helping you?"

"Yep, they really want to do this with me . . . and keep me company." I remember adults do not want me to be alone.

I make a mental note to let Roberto and Maya know that we are doing the project together.

"Well, I wanted you to do this project individually."

I put on my sad face.

"But I guess it is never too early for you kids to practice teamwork."

"Great!" I say eagerly. "We can work on it after school before we go home."

I know this will throw off Auntie Mabel's plan to pick me up. She has to be home later in the day to babysit some kindergarten kids. She will not be able to walk me home now.

* * *

During recess I go to see Ms. Bridges, our school librarian, to show her the pictures I took of the garbage truck in Stinky Dump. Roberto and Maya are with me. They were not having it when I first told them about us partnering on the project.

"Ms. Allie wants us to do the project as a group thing," I told them.

Maya is suspicious. "Ms. Allie said we have to do it individually."

"Okay," I admit. "Mom and Dad and the teachers want me to be around people. Help a brother out."

At that, they both nod in agreement.

"Do you have a topic?" asks Maya.

"Oh yeah. I sure do."

Roberto sounds happy. "So you are going to do the project for us!"

Maya nods in agreement with Roberto.

"No," I say. "We are going to do the project together, as a team."

Their faces drop. Maya says, "But if it is your idea, why do we have to do it?"

"It's cool! You will love it. We are going to investigate what is really going on at Stinky Dump."

That sounds exciting to both Roberto and Maya. "Yeah! Let's do it."

So now here we are in the library. Ms. Bridges is energetic and usually wears colorful African headbands. "You gotta remember your roots," she always says.

Ms. Bridges calls us over when we enter the library. Now she puts a hand on my shoulder. "How have you been doing, JR? Look, wait over here, and I will be right back to talk to you." She rubs my shoulder as she leaves.

"She is being really nice to you," notes Roberto.

"Well, you know adults talk about us all the time. I am sure they talk about my little sister."

"And then they go tell your parents," says Maya.

Roberto and I nod in agreement.

"But you're okay, right, JR?" asks Roberto.

"I'm okay. I feel great. Never been better."

"You've been biting your nails a lot," remarks Maya. She takes the opportunity to show off her perfectly polished nails. She always complains that the school will not allow her to have fancy designs, just basic nail polish.

Ms. Bridges returns. "So how can I help you guys today?"

Everybody looks at me—Roberto, Maya, and Ms. Bridges.

I suddenly realize the seriousness of the moment. I try to talk, but I start choking up. Finally, I say, "Ms. Bridges, my family is in danger."

All three look at me like I am crazy.

I control my breathing and continue. "Remember you were telling us about all the nuclear garbage that is out there?"

Ms. Bridges nods.

"Well, this empty lot has some of it. If I don't stop it, it will kill my whole family."

My two ride-or-die partners rally 'round and start supporting me.

"We call it Stinky Dump," says Roberto.

"It smells awful," says Maya.

"Uhm . . . why do you think it has nu—okay, what proof do you have about the nuclear waste?"

"Well, Ms. Bridges, I want to show you these." I show her my phone with the pictures of the red garbage bags.

"Whoa!" Ms. Bridges screws up her face as if an awful smell just hit her. She grabs hold of the phone and does not let go. "Are those red garbage bags? Is that medical waste? Where did you get this picture?"

I am immediately suspicious. "I dunno." I do not let go of the phone and do not show her the other pictures of the truck's license plate. We both tug at the phone until Ms. Bridges gives up and lets me keep it.

Ms. Bridges looks at the other two, and they shrug their shoulders, pretending to be ignorant just like me.

"Soon they will be putting radioactive waste in the garbage, if they haven't done that already," says Ms. Bridges.

"That sounds dangerous," says Roberto.

"It is! Many people have been killed by radioactive and other contaminated waste. They die slow and painful deaths."

My mind flashes back to my little sister's short life. She was always sickly with many things, including asthma. However, she then got leukemia, and that was really bad. Joan's autoimmune deficiency meant she could not fight illnesses as well as other people. I remember the feeling of helplessness I had when the doctors said Joan's leukemia was very severe and she could lose her life at any time. There were some close calls, and then the worst thing we could ever imagine happened, and eight-year-old Joan died.

"So toxic waste causes you to catch a disease?" I am intrigued.

"Well, it is not like one disease that you catch, but if you hang around areas with a lot of toxins, your body is less able to fight off any diseases that might come around."

"Like the nuclear waste in that exhibit you are putting together?"

"Well, yeah! Sort of. Radioactive waste, nuclear waste, other garbage, it will always affect you."

Did I hear NUCLEAR GARBAGE? So that is what the guys in Stinky Dump are trying to hide! And it is right next to me and my family.

I try to sound as innocent as possible. "If I told you the address of Stinky Dump, would you be able to tell me who owns it?"

Roberto and Maya stiffen for a moment as if frightened, but then they relax and smile. They remember the last time I got them involved in asking Ms. Bridges for help. All the adults in the family had made a big fuss over Junior going to Howard University. I did not know anything about Howard University, and neither did Roberto or Maya. We asked Ms. Bridges, and she made us do the research ourselves. So she was not helpful at all, as we had to do the work on our own. But she showed us how to research it and made a point to have us tell her what we learned. It turned out to be very interesting and well worth the effort, and that is why Roberto and Maya smile when remembering it.

We learned that Howard University is a university in Washington, DC, and that it started way, way, way, way back in 1867. It is an HBCU. We looked that up—it means Historically Black Colleges and Universities, which were formed just after the American Civil War, when Black students were not allowed to attend predominantly white universities. There are about a hundred HBCUs, mostly in the southern United States, and Junior insisted that Howard University is the finest one. Ms. Bridges made us go back and do more research (*sigh!*) on some of the famous people who had attended Howard University, and it was a very long list.

We hope that Ms. Bridges will be more helpful this time, even though the Howard University research turned out to be fun.

Ms. Bridges walks away and beckons for us to follow her.

"I think she is actually going to help us this time," whispers Roberto into one of my ears, and I nod in agreement.

"I think it is because you had a death in your family recently," whispers Maya into my other ear. While I do not nod in agreement with this, I silently believe that it is true.

Ms. Bridges sits us down around a computer and starts typing away on the Internet. She talks to us as she types. "All of this is public information and can be found if you know where to look."

She takes us to a real estate listing website, but it is no help. "Maybe the property has not changed ownership recently," Ms. Bridges explains. So she goes to what she says is a New York State database, and, sure enough, there is the property and the owner listed right there.

"Who is 'REB NYC New York LLC'?" I ask. "What kind of name is that?"

Ms. Bridges explains it is a corporation and not a real person. "This sounds like a real estate developer. They are trying to hide their real identity. We will check the state business registry, but I'm sure they used a lawyer to form the corporation, so we still won't know their name."

Ms. Bridges goes onto another New York State website, and, sure enough, there is the real name of the owner of Stinky Dump.

"This must be a really cheap developer," says Ms. Bridges. "So cheap they didn't even hire a lawyer to form their corporation. Instead, they did it themselves."

I look at the name that Ms. Bridges has printed out for us. Kaston Dagoul, REB NYC New York LLC, and it is at 39 West 40th Street in Manhattan.

I have found the owner of Stinky Dump.

I must find a way to stop this person from doing more harm.

CHAPTER 8

I TELL THE STORY TO MY FRIENDS.

Roberto and Maya lean in as I finish. "... and then I hear my dad say, 'Let us see if he can handle this visit to the museum. Then we will know he is mature enough to walk home and do more on his own.'"

We are approaching the subway stop near school. Two days before, Ms. Bridges told us there was a movie at the Brooklyn Museum about environmental problems facing the Earth. I convinced Ms. Allie that it was extremely important that we saw the movie for our project.

"But it's only showing in the morning, JR. That's school time. What about it is important?"

I was ready with an answer, because not only had I read about it, but I had also read what the critics wrote about it. Apparently, critics are people who go around hating on movies and other stuff and then write what they think.

I end with "Ask Ms. Bridges. She is the one who says we should see it." My hands are behind my back with my fingers crossed. I hope she does not ask Ms. Bridges for details.

"Remember," I add, "all three of us need to go so I will not be alone."

* * *

Ms. Bridges and Ms. Allie talked about it. They were the best of friends and were always talking to each other. We just wanted permission to get out of school for a day to "further our knowledge," as Roberto put it. The Brooklyn Museum was just a few subway stops from school, and Maya reminded Ms. Allie about the school's mission, or some such thing, to produce independent children who thrive and stuff like that.

Then they got permission from the school. They even contacted a buddy they had at the museum—they called him a liaison—who would take care of us (and snitch if we did something wrong, I guess).

Then they told our parents. Mom was not really having it, but Dad came through.

So now that I have gotten us out of school for the day, my two friends consider me a hero. Little do they know I have other plans in mind as well.

The movie is really good! Better than I expected from an educational movie. It shows how the Earth is being destroyed by climate change and environmental disasters. Millions of kids get contaminated and die each year because of illness from chemical dumping grounds. "I'm now surer than ever that Stinky Dump contaminated and killed my sister," I say.

"You have the proof: pictures of red garbage bags," explains Maya.

After the movie, my friends think I am brilliant when I say we should do further research by visiting the offices of Kaston Dagoul in Manhattan. We consider it crucial to our project and think we can justify it if we are caught.

We decide that before we go to midtown Manhattan, we will walk around downtown Brooklyn by the Barclays Center. We get off the subway at the Atlantic Avenue/Barclays Center station to find a lot of activity: shoppers, vehicles, pedestrians, workers, tourists, every type of person you can find in the world, moving through the high-rise buildings and busy streets. We see why this has become the busiest part of Brooklyn.

Afterwards, we hop on the Number 2, 3 train to the Bronx and get off at Times Square. As usual, I enjoy the experience of the subway ride: the excitement of walking down the stairs to go underground, the noise of the approaching train, the subway car full of people. We could have gotten off closer to the developer's offices on the east side of Manhattan, but we figured that as we were in the area, we should do a quick detour through Times Square. Times Square is busy as usual, but we manage to stay on schedule, more or less, despite the distractions.

We arrive at the address. It is a tall building, and the developer's office is in it. We check the board that lists all the companies in the building. The developer's office, REB NY NEW YORK LLC, is on the 7th floor. This is exciting! Oops, there is a security guard behind a desk, but he is doing something on his phone. However, people are just walking past him, and no one is checking in or showing him ID.

We decide to play it cool, like we belong in the building.

"Let's have a cover story in case someone stops us," says Maya, always thinking like a detective.

"We should say one of our parents works on the 7th floor and we came by so they can take us to . . ." I try to think of where the imaginary parent on the 7th floor wants to take us.

"An audition for a kid's play on Broadway. Broadway theaters are within walking distance, and people in Manhattan are always pushing their kids to be in things like that," says Maya.

We all nod and agree. Each of us has at one time or another been victimized by a parent who wanted us to get "culture" by playing an instrument or a sport or something. I shudder as I remember the time my mom thought I should take piano lessons. Judging from Roberto's and Maya's reactions, they are also reliving some past trauma related to this subject.

We first try to walk past the security desk as if we belong. It works. We join a group of adults—returning from lunch, I expect—and walk right by the texting security guard. Our school has better security than this.

This is too exciting, and we get even more nervous as we approach the entry to the office. We expected one of those fancy offices like you see in

TV shows and movies. Instead, the inside of the building is old, dark, and depressing. There is no glass-doored entryway with well-dressed, happy people moving around briskly. There is a metal door, one of many in the corridor, with a peephole.

After we ring the doorbell, someone apparently looks through the peephole. A muffled voice says, "Oh! Do I have to sign for it?"

We do not know how to respond, and we simply look at each other. The door opens and a woman sticks her head out. She looks about age thirty or so, I guess. It's hard to judge the ages of adults once they get past twenty-one.

"Oh! You're kids. That's why I didn't see you through the peephole. Sorry!" She covers her mouth as she apologizes.

We say hello, but she is already on to her next sentence. "So what are you selling? Not more candy, I hope. I'm trying to go on a diet."

I take the lead. "We wanted to talk to you about the nuclear garbage on one of your properties."

"Oh! I don't own any properties, honey. I'm just a temp. I'm a starving artist." She looks at her watch. "As a matter of fact, I have an audition and have to leave soon, so . . ." She makes a motion with her hand that we should speed things along.

The three of us are in sync, and we automatically turn on the charm.

"Oh, are you an actress?" gushes Maya.

"Are you famous?" says Roberto, wide-eyed.

"Can we have your autograph?" I plead.

She blushes and accepts the praise. "Oh, no, I'm not famous! Not yet. Come on in."

We enter, and she goes around a desk and reaches for her purse.

We stop her. "We are not selling anything. We just want to ask the owner of the piece of land next to my house to stop dumping nuclear garbage on it. It is killing my family," I explain.

She does not understand. I choke up before I can even start the sentence. Why do I always choke up like I am going to cry whenever I talk about Stinky Dump and what it has done to my family?

"What is the address?" she asks.

We tell her, and she writes it down on a piece of paper. We introduce ourselves, and she takes down our names also.

"Shouldn't you be in school, though?" She seems genuinely concerned about this, and we hem and haw without directly answering the question.

"School is out now," says Maya.

We tell her the school we go to, and she also writes that down.

She nods. "My boss is such a scumbag. I totally believe you."

I add, "Your boss is a simpleton."

"The waste even killed JR's little sister," adds Maya, and I nod in agreement.

The temp is shocked. "Oh my! You poor thing." She reaches over and rubs my shoulder. She says she really has no power and explains again that she is a temporary employee.

"I know absolutely nothing about the actual running of the business," she says. "But I will have a conversation with the owner when he returns. I cannot be part of an organization that behaves like this."

"Who is the owner? What is his name?" asks Roberto with a really big smile planted on his face, even though we already know his name.

She writes down the owner's name and gives it to us. We leave feeling satisfied because she has said she will act on it. As we descend in the elevator, we evaluate the meeting. Roberto says, "I don't think she is a bad person."

Oh no, Roberto has a crush on her! Maya and I look at each other and roll our eyes.

"Let's focus on business," I remark. "Okay, Roberto?" Roberto is the last one I had imagined would need help focusing.

Upon exiting the office building, we talk about how long we can spend in Times Square and get away with it. It isn't often that we end up in the tourist capital of the world. So much to do! So much to see! So little time!

We instinctively walk in the direction of Times Square. Maya is the only one of us who has been to an actual Broadway show, and she wants to show us the building. Times Square is said to be the crossroads of the world, and there is always a crowded and positive vibe nestled among the tall buildings. Tourists, workers, performers—it is always exciting, like the subway. Roberto has recently read about some street performers who are really exciting, and he wants to look for them.

"I hear they are much better than that 'it's showtime' stuff you get when riding the subway," Roberto says. My dad often complains about those guys.

We also vote and decide to get something to eat. Maya comments about Roberto and me always being hungry.

"I have some money from Dad's friend who came by," I tell them. "I think I'll get some souvenirs for Junior and Ayesha."

"Won't they ask where you got the souvenirs?" says Roberto. Roberto always has money and is considered our numbers guy. He always gets interested when we speak about money.

"I will tell them to just shut up and accept the gift. See how nice I am to them even after all the mean things they have done to me?"

My friends nod in agreement. We swap stories about how mean my older brother and sister are to me as we set off to buy them gifts.

Freedom and Times Square—what could be better?

CHAPTER 9

THE NEXT DAY, WE ARE BACK AT school as normal. The other kids are so jealous that we got off school to see a movie. They hate us! Haha!

I run into Roberto and Maya, and we are still excited about our adventure the day before, plus I may have solved the problem of Stinky Dump if the temp worker we met comes through for us. So we are walking down the hallway, recalling details of the trip. We are also trying to persuade Roberto that it is not necessary to return for a follow-up visit to thank the temporary worker.

Then we get a shock. The public address system mentions each of our names.

We stop walking, and we don't move a muscle as we wait for the announcement to finish. After calling our names twice, the announcement ends with: "Please report to the principal's office immediately."

Kids walking past stare at us with looks of pity. It is never a good thing being told to go see the principal "immediately." We look at each other with surprise, turn, and begin a sullen trudge toward the principal's office.

As is usual in these circumstances, there are soft chants of "Dead man walking" from my simpleton schoolmates. A no-talent simpleton starts beatboxing for the occasion:

> Dead man (*1, 2*) walking (*3, 4*)
> Dead man (*1, 2*) walking (*3, 4*)
> Dead man (*1, 2*) walking (*3, 4*)

It is definitely more fun when you are doing the chanting.

We wait to see Principal Fletcher (my nickname for her is "Judge-and-Jury"). We take the opportunity to ask her always-cheerful assistant what mood the principal is in today. We get back a positive reply.

We do not have to wait long. Judge-and-Jury appears, then insists on having a prolonged conversation about how we are doing. Are we enjoying school, she asks.

We grunt back, barely audibly replying that all is fine in our worlds.

Finally, she ushers us into the office and closes the door behind us.

Judge-and-Jury ignores us for a few seconds as she finishes typing something into her computer. *Perhaps she has already decided on a punishment and is typing it into the school's punishment system,* I think. After she finishes typing, she looks at us and gets right to the point. "Did the three of you skip class yesterday?"

"Skip?"

"Why do you ask us that?"

"I dunno."

Our responses are not helping us. *We should have done a little planning on our way here.*

"I don't understand what you guys are saying," says Judge-and-Jury.

We are saved when the assistant pokes her head into the room. Principal Fletcher's presence is needed elsewhere, urgently. As she gets up to hurry out, she tells her assistant, "Call their parents and have them come in first thing tomorrow."

The three of us stiffen.

As I mull over the issues, I come to the realization that members of my crew have been boasting about skipping out after the movie and going to

Manhattan. I told only two or three people, but Roberto and Maya must have told everyone in the world.

We look at each other as Principal Fletcher leaves the room. We later decide to tell our parents that we have no idea why they are being asked to come to school.

It is going to be a nail-biting night. School meetings are already becoming painful for parents, as there is now a school meeting for everything. However, I am beginning to have visions of my freedom being taken away again. I will then be subjected to walking home with Auntie Mabel and the kindergarten kids for the rest of my life.

* * *

That evening, I stay in my room and pretend to be doing homework and studying. My parents have been planning to wait me out and ambush me when I go downstairs to get something to eat. However, they realize they are losing that battle, and they call me downstairs to the living room.

I try to finesse the situation by asking, "What for?" from the relative safety of my bedroom. This angers them, and they yell at me to come downstairs "right now."

I trudge reluctantly down the stairs.

In these situations, they usually put me to sit on the other side of the coffee table. The coffee table creates a barrier and that "us versus them" feeling. I think this makes it easier for them to inflict punishment; they feel as if I am their opponent when I am sitting on the opposite side of the coffee table. So I take the initiative and rush to sit between them on the couch. Now it feels like we are on the same side, literally and figuratively.

My dad gets right to the point. "Your school called us in. Why do I have to show up at your school?"

My mom kicks in. "Give the baby a chance."

Normally I would not like the 'baby' reference, but I am happy about it this time as I think it bodes well for my fate.

"I think we should both go, given what JR is going through," Mom says.

"Sure, I agree," replies Dad. "So, JR, why are we rearranging our work schedules to go to your school tomorrow?"

I do not lie, as I do not like lying. "I am not sure what it is about. I heard they called in some other kids' parents, too. Maybe they are eventually going to call in everyone."

I do not think this is lying, because I would bet you two Knicks tickets that every single kid in that school will, at one time or another, have their parents dragged down to the school for some unnecessary meeting.

My parents eye me suspiciously. I use my best innocent face. It is better that they find out at the meeting about the allegations of my skipping school. If they find out now, they will just spend the night tossing and turning, like me.

When I am released, I stop by the kitchen to eat as I am already close to it. I quickly locate an unfinished bag of chips captive in the kitchen cabinet and liberate it.

Junior and Ayesha pass through the kitchen and ask me what that was all about. I know that Ayesha is making inquiries to find out what trouble I am in, no doubt hoping to learn something she can use against me. They also ask me more questions about where I got the souvenirs I gave them. Hopefully those will produce some goodwill, along with the chips I generously offer them. It is going to be an anxious night for me.

CHAPTER 10

THE NEXT MORNING, OUR ANNOYED PARENTS SHOW up to the conference room outside Principal Fletcher's office. We watch them come in: both of my parents; Roberto's dad, Mr. Rodriguez; and Deacon Jackson—that is what Maya's mom is called around our neighborhood. Deacon Jackson was a deacon at a local church before going into politics, and she still introduces herself as Deacon Jackson.

I believe it is a good thing that our parents are here. The more adults there are in the room, the more likely there will be conflict among them, decreasing the chance of us kids being punished.

We three kids are anxious, but we put up a brave face, or at least we fake looks of 'I am innocent, so that is why I am barely paying attention.'

We were texting each other last night:

(Roberto) Our parents have been called to the school so much that they are beginning to not take it seriously.

(Me) If you become breathless walking up the stairs, they would call your parents in.

(Maya) My mom says that schools do not have enough resources.

> **(Me)** My dad says how in his day you had to be on your last breath before the school would summon the nurse or call 911.

While we wait for Principal Fletcher, instead of discussing the trouble their kids are causing, our parents socialize and discuss other topics.

First, Deacon Jackson and Mr. Rodriguez hug and console my parents. Joan's passing is still fresh in everyone's mind.

After that, my mom gushes to Deacon Jackson, Maya's mother, "Oh, that diet you have me on is amazing."

"Oh, isn't it? It is making such a difference for me also."

I am pleased for three reasons: my mom does not stay on these diets for long, my mom does not require any other family member to be on the same diet, and they are not discussing our misbehavior…alleged misbehavior.

Meanwhile, my dad and Mr. Rodriguez fall into a glum discussion about the state of the New York Knicks and then brighten up at the thought of the next fishing season approaching.

Judge-and-Jury's meetings are running late. There are another student and parent in front of us.

Mr. Rodriguez complains, "This is like waiting at a doctor's office."

Deacon Jackson says, "I doubt it is Principal Fletcher's fault. The way the school board focuses on the wrong things, bothering principals for every little infraction . . . it's shameful."

My dad goes back to one of his pet issues. "Everyone is worried about liability these days. Down at MTA, they make us write up everything. A drunk passenger ran into a closing door trying to catch a train the other day and sued. Conductor and motorman spent hours writing up reports. The lawyers even had them in a deposition."

Deacon Jackson is surprised. She says, "Oh my! It went that far?" as my dad nods.

My mom chimes in. "I feel bad for the teachers. All the things they have to go through. Then they catch a lawsuit."

Mr. Rodriguez shakes his head. "True! I guess that's why they called us down here for our kids' infractions."

"*Alleged* infractions," says Roberto.

Mr. Rodriguez glares at him, and I think for a moment that Roberto is about to catch a beatdown, but the moment passes safely.

Eventually we are all called into Judge-and-Jury's office.

When we sit, Deacon Jackson immediately takes charge. "So what is this about?"

Principal Fletcher—Judge-and-Jury—replies: "Oh, first I wanted to have a conversation with you about the garbage piling up at the corner by the school." Knowing that Deacon Jackson is a local politician, Principal Fletcher cannot let an opportunity pass to get something for her school.

"Which agency? Sanitation?"

"I think so."

Deacon Jackson asks a few questions and then goes on a rant. "The city agencies should be reacting positively to school needs. The DOT should be taking care of that road, and DOS should be doing maintenance . . ." My brother Junior later told me that those letters were called acronyms. DOT stands for Department of Transportation, DOS for Department of Sanitation.

They are about to get into something about the education budget when the other parents cough, quietly, the polite way adults do when they want to get someone's attention.

Deacon Jackson takes the hint. "Yes, this meeting is for other issues, but let me tell you, if it were up to me, increasing resources for schools would be THE top priority."

The adults nod politely. We kids wonder what the hell that was all about.

Deacon Jackson returns to the reason for the meeting. "So I thought the kids had permission to go to the movie at the museum."

My parents smile. Mom gushes, "Oh, yes—we were so happy JR was able to do that without any problem." She turns to Mr. Rodriguez and puts her hand on his shoulder. "You know, he has not been himself since his little sister passed away, so we are keeping an eye on him."

I am embarrassed. "Mom, you said not to discuss family business in public."

Dad gets in on the act. "He certainly showed he can handle more responsibility."

Principal Fletcher listens politely. "The problem was not the movie. Apparently, after the movie, your kids ended up in Manhattan. Your kids skipped school. Truancy is the word we used back in the day."

I sense that Judge-and-Jury wants to be on Deacon Jackson's good side. Yep, just in case Deacon Jackson ever gets to be in power or is in charge of New York City. Being kids, we pick up on this immediately. Maya's mom has power because she is involved with local politics. We nod at each other, and smiles cross our faces.

Maya is on it. "But you all said we could go to investigate for the project!" Roberto and I nod vigorously.

Judge-and-Jury will not let it go. "Your three little angels here were apparently caught skipping school after the museum."

A few days later, Roberto told my big brother, Junior, that he was flattered the principal called us angels. Junior explained to the three of us that Judge-and-Jury was using something called sarcasm, and that she actually meant we were the opposite of angels, more like the devil in kids' bodies. "You little kids don't get sarcasm," my brother said.

Anyway, the adults stare at us kids as if they expect us to say something.

Roberto insists, "How are we going to get our project done if we cannot do research?"

The adults do not appear to be convinced. It is at this moment—the darkest moment of our school careers—that Principal Fletcher's phone rings. I foresee Auntie Mabel walking me home when I'm a senior in college.

Principal Fletcher picks up the call. "Yes?"

She listens for a moment. Then then her face fills with real, real anger. Not the type of anger when one of us kids does something wrong, but many times that.

"What is he doing here? No, he cannot come in here. Who does he think he is?"

Principal Fletcher puts the call on hold, then composes herself. She turns to our parents. "That was the person who complained to the mayor's office about your children's truancy. The district superintendent wants me to try and work with him. Name is Kaston Dagoul."

Deacon Jackson leans forward intently. "What? Something is fishy here. Who is he?"

I chime in. "He owns Stinky Dump."

The adults do not know what Stinky Dump is. I explain that it is the empty lot next to our house. My parents, Deacon Jackson, and Mr. Rodriguez all know the spot; they nod knowingly. Judge-and-Jury still looks a little perplexed.

Principal Fletcher continues. "He says he is a real estate developer. I told my assistant he cannot be in our meeting."

"But he made the complaint," says Mr. Rodriguez.

"You know what? I would like to have him in our meeting," my dad says.

The other parents nod in agreement.

Principal Fletcher looks anxious. "That is not protocol."

Deacon Jackson stops her. "We are the parents. We want to meet him. We have your back."

A few seconds after Principal Fletcher picks up the call again and whispers into the phone, Kaston Dagoul bursts through the door.

I stare at the man who killed my little sister.

CHAPTER 11

I WANT TO SAY SOMETHING TO KASTON Dagoul, but instead I continue to stare at him.

I whisper to Roberto and Maya, "I cannot believe I am in the same room as the guy who killed my sister." They reach out and touch me on the shoulder, thinking I am going to lose it and go crazy. They must have seen something in the way I stare at Kaston Dagoul.

I do not like him. Kaston Dagoul is a weaselly-looking guy. He's only just entered the room, and he's already acting as if he owns it.

I continue to stare at him.

He reaches over and shakes hands with Principal Fletcher but no one else. Deacon Jackson is offended and seethes.

Then Kaston Dagoul hands Principal Fletcher a business card and gets to talking. "I am very busy, so I do not have a lot of time for this."

Roberto says to his dad, "Papa, didn't you say it is rude to enter a room and not shake everyone's hand?"

"Yes, that is exactly what I said, son," replies Mr. Rodriguez.

The developer slows his roll and shakes everyone's hand.

Except mine. I just stare at his hand as if it is . . . nuclear garbage.

My mom and dad nudge me to shake his hand, but I fold my arms and shake my head, still just staring at him. Kaston Dagoul looks at my hateful stare and wisely decides to move on.

He is offered a seat but refuses it, instead standing over everyone. He looks at us with a raised eyebrow.

Principal Fletcher tries to assert control. "Let's do this step by step. This meeting is not supposed to be happening, but the district office says you are a concerned taxpayer—"

Maya's mom interrupts. "More like a concerned lobbyist. Don't I know your name from somewhere?"

Principal Fletcher interjects. "Let one person speak at a time. Let the developer speak first."

I immediately notice that the principal did not call him by name, but instead he was "the developer." *Nice!*

The developer speaks. "I was told by my assistant—*one* of my assistants, that is—that a group of kids showed up on our premises making allegations about a plot of land I own." He gives the address of Stinky Dump. Yes, this is definitely the guy who owns Stinky Dump.

"Hey, that is the lot right next to our house," says my dad.

"Oh, right," says my mom. "The one that smells so bad. Why don't you clean it up?"

Deacon Jackson jumps in. "I know that lot. I have been trying to get it cleaned up for years."

Everyone stares at the developer. He stammers. "Yes, right now I am in the process of cleaning up . . . the city agencies are preventing me from . . . it costs a lot of money to clean up a mess left by the previous owner."

"Ah! Money. You don't want to spend the money to clean it up," Mr. Rodriguez says while nodding at Roberto. They are both very numbers oriented.

Roberto nods back at his dad.

The developer puffs out his chest. "That is not the topic of our conversation. Your kids harassed my assistant!"

The principal suddenly gets interested. "Oh my! Were they threatening? Please tell us what happened. Can your assistant make a statement?"

"Oh. A statement. Well, she said they were well behaved. I believe she used the word *cute*."

Maya and I glance over in time to catch Roberto blushing.

"Anyway, that assistant is no longer employed by my company."

Roberto asks weakly, "Do you know where she went to?" but he is ignored.

The principal nods. "So you are here about the truancy issue."

"I am here because they were trespassing on my property. Plus, they allege that I am responsible for killing people."

The other adults are confused.

I decide I will say my piece, damn the consequences. "He owns Stinky Dump. He killed my little sister."

I suddenly realize I am standing with my fists clenched. I do not know how I got to be in that position, but here I am. I am choked up, the same way I always get when I talk about my sister and Stinky Dump. Also, I realize that I am shaking with anger and out of breath, almost shouting.

Okay, not "almost." I am in fact shouting, and everyone in the room is looking at me with concern.

I start over, trying to control my temper this time but without much luck. I end up pointing at the developer. "This simpleton—developer, whatever—put nuclear garbage in Stinky Dump, and it killed my little sister."

I do not think I have ever felt so out of control before.

My dad puts his hand on my shoulder and tenderly pulls me back toward my seat while Mom reaches out and lowers my finger, which is still pointing at the developer.

I finally sit, and my mom puts her hand around my shoulder to calm me down. "It's rude to point."

The developer chimes in. "What did you call my property?"

"Stinky Dump!" all three of us kids yell back at the same time.

My dad adds, "Yep! It does smell awful."

The developer tries to continue. "Anyway, they came in threatening."

We roll our eyes.

My mom points out, "You just said they were well behaved. We have always trained our kids to have good manners."

"'Threatening' as in they were going to hurt someone?" asks Mr. Rodriguez.

"Well, no. Threatening as in they are going to report me."

Deacon Jackson: "Report you for what?"

I answer for the developer. "Stinky Dump."

The principal adds, "It is a very serious charge to accuse someone of threatening. Making threats is a crime."

Deacon Jackson responds. "Threatening! Yes, that is very different." She turns to the developer. "What is going on at Stinky Dump?"

Great! We have her using our name—Stinky Dump!

Kaston Dagoul stammers, "Nothing is going on . . . and they were trespassing." He has a lightbulb moment. "Trespassing is a felony!"

Maya, our future detective, is ready with an answer. "Trespassing is only a misdemeanor."

"But they were not rude in any way?" my mom asks again.

"Again, no, they were actually very well behaved," the developer says. "But they should have been in school."

My mom looks flattered that her son is 'well behaved.'

Judge-and-Jury replies, "The school will take care of that." She glances ominously in our direction, then back to Kaston Dagoul, who begins to grumble about suing everyone involved.

Deacon Jackson is becoming even more annoyed. "Sue who? You plan to sue a school because some of their kids skipped school?"

My dad finally speaks up. "You should have just told us," he says to the developer, "and we would have taken care of it."

Kaston Dagoul tries a different tack. "My business is not doing anything illegal. Why did they come to see me?"

"Because this place you own, Stinky Dump, is apparently a nuisance, and they thought that coming to talk to you was their only recourse," concludes Mr. Rodriguez.

I see Judge-and-Jury nodding in agreement with Mr. Rodriguez. *Nice,* I think to myself. *Principal Fletcher is not a totally lost cause.* This gives me some more courage to speak up. "We were trying to stop him from dumping more nuclear garbage in Stinky Dump."

I am pleased with myself, as I did not shake and have a tantrum this time.

"Extortion!" yells the developer. I do not know what that is and will have to look up the meaning.

After some more back-and-forth, Principal Fletcher tells the developer to leave us alone, but in a nice way. "The school will handle this."

Kaston Dagoul, the developer, leaves in a huff, still mumbling about suing everyone in the school until we lose our houses and all our kids live on the street. This concerns us kids a lot, but we are reassured by the rolling eyes and smirks on the faces of the other adults.

Kaston Dagoul's parting words are: "If it is the last thing I do, I will take your houses, and you will all be living in homeless shelters. I will then rent out your houses . . ."—he thinks for a second—". . . at market rates."

Kaston Dagoul slams the door on his way out. We are left alone with our parents and Principal Fletcher. I hope the developer catches a disease from the nuclear garbage at Stinky Dump.

Judge-and-Jury rubs her hands together and speaks to the room. "Now we have to decide on a proper punishment for these infractions." I personally think she was rubbing her hands too gleefully at the thought of punishing us. I mean, it is supposed to be a solemn moment, not a time for celebration.

Deacon Jackson steps up. "This lawsuit stuff is bullshit!" Strong language! I know that sometime in the future my mom will refer to this as an example of Deacon Jackson's lack of parenting skills.

Deacon Jackson continues, "I know about this developer. He has projects in our neighborhood, but he has never contributed to any of my campaigns. He only gives to the big shots. He must be doing something evil if he showed up here at the school the very next day, acting all guilty and defensive."

Judge-and-Jury tries to get the meeting back on track. "Let's focus on the punishment."

Deacon Jackson is not having it. "Any punishment may be seen as weakness on our part if he makes good on his threat to sue."

Roberto, Maya, and I all nod in agreement. My parents and Mr. Rodriguez look to Principal Fletcher for guidance. Judge-and-Jury quickly calculates that Deacon Jackson would be a good person to have on her side, and we can see her rethinking the concept of punishing us.

Winning!

CHAPTER 12

"YOU HAVE TO CHOOSE A NEW PROJECT for class."

Ms. Allie jumps the three of us later to deliver the bad news. "This project is causing too much trouble. Plus, you took advantage of it to skip school."

Ms. Allie did not listen to our point that we did not technically skip school. "Your parents, Principal Fletcher, Ms. Bridges, and I decided this is the best thing to do," she said.

With that, she stalks off, leaving the three of us sulking.

"These adults do not understand how dangerous Stinky Dump is," I say. "It took my sister, and next it will take other members of my family, and then the whole neighborhood."

"This is serious," says Roberto.

"It is going to kill us off one at a time," adds Maya.

* * *

Aha! The idea comes to me as I am resting my chin on my hand and gazing out my bedroom window again, unable to daydream or sleep.

For the rest of the night, I think about my idea and refine it so that I can present it to Roberto and Maya tomorrow.

After I tell them my idea, they are excited, but they still try to strike a better deal for themselves.

"It sounds like a lot of work," complains Roberto.

"Yep. I have a lot of things on my plate," sighs Maya. "I'm not sure if I can manage that."

"Look, my family is the one in the most immediate danger, so I'm willing to do most of the work."

As soon as those words come from my mouth, they announce they can "work with me" to get it done.

We seek out Ms. Allie right away. "We have the perfect idea for a new class project, Ms. Allie," we explain.

Just like an adult, Ms. Allie immediately tries to take control of our project, but then she gives in. "This is highly unusual, but seeing how JR has been under a lot of stress, I will allow it."

"I am not stressed. I am good. I am fine. Never been better."

Ms. Allie ignores me and continues. "Every Monday, Wednesday, and Friday, you must give me an oral progress report, especially on what you plan to do next. I do not want you sneaking off to Manhattan again."

The three of us are about to respond and defend ourselves, but based on the way Ms. Allie stares at us, we decide to let it go. Ms. Allie also says our project can be in the form of an oral presentation rather than a written report that is pages and pages and pages and pages long.

That last part is a huge win for us, and we will run with it.

CHAPTER 13

WE MUST GET AUNTIE MABEL ON BOARD.

"Let me deal with Auntie Mabel," I say to Roberto and Maya confidently.

That afternoon, I see Auntie Mabel coddling the flowers in her small front yard. I saunter on over nonchalantly, say hello, and ask if she needs help.

Auntie Mabel says, "No. I got this." Then she looks at me suspiciously as I sit casually on her stoop and smile at her.

The expression on her face says, *Hmm!* She realizes that something is up. I change my seating position to be even more casual and stretch my legs out. Auntie Mabel wipes some dirt off a flower and is becoming amused. Just like an adult, she is not taking me seriously. So I pull my legs up and cross them to look more mature. It is not a comfortable position for me, and I know my discomfort is showing on my face.

"What do you want, JR?" Auntie Mabel asks. "Are you hungry?"

I am hungry, but I'm mature enough to get past that for now. I come clean and run my idea past her: school project, community-oriented, surprise street welcome for her son when he returns home from his Army deployment.

She does not love it! There is a lot of hemming and hawing about unforeseen consequences: noise, some stranger wanting to use her bathroom, emergency vehicles not being able to get through the street.

I tell her that Ms. Allie thinks it is a great idea. I base this on the fact that Ms. Allie said we could give it a try.

Then Malcolm shows up. Auntie Mabel and I greet him warmly, and he stops to talk.

Auntie Mabel puts down the plants she has been holding and gives Malcolm a hug. "Congratulations on your high school graduation, Malcolm." She turns to me. "Malcolm is the first one from his family to graduate from high school."

"Well, I think I have some cousins over in the Bronx who have GEDs," responds Malcolm humbly.

Auntie Mabel rubs her hands together and beams at Malcolm. "Now it's off into the world. The world is yours, young man."

Malcolm smiles again. "Actually, I wanted to thank you for the letter of recommendation. I got accepted into the auto mechanic school. And thanks for all the advice."

"You thanked me already, Malcolm."

Malcolm looks over at me. "I am going to your place later, JR, to thank your dad for his letter of recommendation."

"De nada," I reply.

In truth, my dad had sweated over that recommendation letter as if Malcolm's entire life depended on it. Junior and Ayesha were called in to advise on technology, fonts, and the best way to use the computer. My mom was recruited to read and edit the letter. Mom has lots of editing advice, and she and Dad ended up arguing over the letter's contents and style. Eventually, they both stalked off in opposite directions, fuming silently and refusing to talk to each other.

I just thought it was nice they were investing so much of their time and emotions to help Malcolm.

Now Malcolm looks at me again. "What are you doing here? Helping Auntie Mabel with her plants?"

"Yes," I reply.

Auntie Mabel rolls her eyes. "JR here has been trying to convince me to help with his school project, a surprise welcome-home party for Jesse."

Malcolm practically explodes. "That's a great idea! When is it? I can borrow a setup and DJ."

Auntie Mabel freezes. I jump in with suggestions. "We can have the DJ booth at the corner by Stinky Dump."

Malcolm agrees and nods. "I have not seen him in ages. You are right to invite everyone to his welcome-home party. No one is going to want to miss that."

Auntie Mabel suddenly warms to the idea. "You know what? Yes! Then everyone can see him at once."

I am distressed that an idea must come from an adult in order for it to be taken seriously. Anyway, Malcolm is already moving on. "Is that dishwasher still working, Auntie Mabel?"

"Oh yes. I do not know what you did, but it is working like a dream."

Whatever works! It looks like we have support from the most important person in my planning. Plus, Malcolm is already promising to help in any way he can.

Great! That means less work for me.

* * *

I immediately call a meeting of the gang, and we meet over at Maya's house. I want to take credit for convincing Auntie Mabel to support our project.

Maya and I sit on the stoop as I retell my heroic story of getting Auntie Mabel on board with the idea of a surprise welcome-home party for her son. I briefly mention Malcolm, but I still take most of the credit. I ask Maya if she has mentioned the welcome-home party to her mom.

Maya replies, "I did. She wants to know who is going to do all the work. Says she is too busy to get caught up in our shenanigans."

"Hmm! Maybe if we get a whole team to barrage her," I say. I think I'm on to something. Seeing as she is a politician, she will be more likely to go along if there is a crowd marching in that direction.

"That would work," says Maya. "But it would take time. And we need to get this done in two or so weeks when Jesse comes home. I told you guys not to wait until the last minute to start a project that we have known about for the whole semester."

I reply, "I think a week or so before the deadline is a reasonable time to start a project." I do not get Maya's reasoning, especially as she went along willingly with what she now calls a delay.

"But it would definitely carry more weight if someone else asked her," says Maya.

"I agree," I say. "I can get my mom and dad to talk to her, and I will see if I can get Auntie Mabel and other adults to drop by and discuss it."

Maya suddenly yells out from her seat on the stoop, "Ma! Ma!" She does it loudly enough that her mother will surely hear her from inside the house. About ten seconds later, a disgusted Deacon Jackson comes out of the front door.

"Why are you shouting for me, Maya? Next time, come into the house and talk to me like a young lady. None of this shouting." She notices me. "Oh! Hello, JR. Are you in trouble again?"

I have been sensing all along that Maya usually blames Roberto and me whenever we get into trouble. I believe Roberto does the same, blaming

Maya and me. I do not take it personally, as I usually do the same, blaming them for taking me down the wrong path in life. It is a system that works for everyone, as we each have to live with the particular adult responsible for setting our punishments.

"Good day, Deacon Jackson. How are you?"

"I'm doing fine, JR. How are your parents and everyone?" She wrings her hands together and looks sad, remembering that they recently lost a child.

I quickly change the subject so another person is not stressed by sadness. "They are well. My mom and Ayesha are loving that new diet you told them about. They say it is making a big difference."

A smile crosses Deacon Jackson's face. "See, Maya? If you stick with the system, it will do wonders for you."

Maya's back is to her mom, and I think I catch her rolling her eyes. Then she says, "Ma, JR says Auntie Mabel is taking part in the welcome home party for Jesse."

"Really? Auntie Mabel would never agree to such a thing!" says a skeptical Deacon Jackson. "Are you sure, JR?"

As I nod, I see Malcolm riding his electric scooter with Roberto. He is giving Roberto a ride. He drops him off in front of Deacon Jackson's house when he sees us. As Roberto comes over, I also wave at Malcolm and gesture for him to join the rest of us.

As Malcolm nears, he speaks to Maya's mom. "Thanks again for that recommendation letter, Deacon Jackson. I don't think I would have gotten into automotive school without it."

"You already thanked me for that, Malcolm. You just work your ass off and make us proud."

Damn! How many recommendations did Malcolm's automotive school application need?

"Isn't it true that Auntie Mabel is helping us set up the welcome-home party?" I ask Malcolm.

Malcolm again becomes animated. "Yes! You gotta jump on this, Deacon Jackson. Auntie Mabel can't wait. She's even thinking of getting news crews and stuff."

Deacon Jackson is suddenly very interested.

"Oh! You know what—maybe I can help out. I should form a committee."

"Can I be on it?" I quickly ask.

"Of course! Let me be the chairperson, as I know proper procedures. Plus, I can get some of the discretionary funds I have control over from the last election cycle. I will put that toward it. Who is in charge of publicity?" she asks Malcolm.

Malcolm shrugs. "I dunno."

"Okay!" comes the quick reply. "I will get my chief of staff and communication group involved. Leave the news crews to me. Some of these news stations are more open to serving the community and politicians than others."

"We will need to have food," I chime in. "Our friend Roberto here is growing and needs to eat." I expect Roberto to thank me for hooking him up with food, but he is distracted by other things.

"Then we'll need a caterer. I have a local person in mind, and we can use the discretionary funds. Let me check with Auntie Mabel on food, though. I don't want to step on anyone's toes."

Malcolm cuts in. "I have to go. I already promised to be the DJ." I believe he is going to meet Junior and the rest of their boring friends.

Deacon Jackson gives Malcolm a raised eyebrow. "We will have to discuss appropriate music for the occasion. Not some of this stuff I hear Maya and her friends listening to."

Maya sighs. Malcolm seizes the opening and leaves.

Deacon Jackson has already pulled out her cell phone and is taking notes. "So I will get my staff to do the planning. I will be the emcee and introduce the speakers." She stops to think, then proceeds with typing again. "DOT . . . DOS . . . local precinct . . . temporary street closures."

Wow! This is turning out too perfectly. Wait until I get them all on the street and they get a whiff of Stinky Dump. They will shut it down immediately.

CHAPTER 14

I THOUGHT OF ALL THE RECOMMENDATIONS THAT Malcolm had to get just to be accepted at his automotive school. I look for him later, as I want a favor from him, but first I ask him how many recommendations he had to get.

Malcolm replies, "Oh, I really only needed one recommendation, and even that was sort of optional."

"Really? Then why did you bother all those people to write recommendations for you?"

"Just to feel the love, JR. Just to feel the love."

We get around to talking about him DJ'ing the Welcome-Home Street Party for Auntie Mabel's son. "Could you tell them they need to have the DJ set-up and the stage right in front of Stinky Dump?"

"Oh, right. That's what you call the empty lot. You certainly branded it. Now everyone is calling it that." I am pleased with this achievement as Malcolm continues, "Why? What do you have up your sleeve?"

"Nothing," I say. "I think my little sister would have appreciated it."

"Sure! I understand. Say no more." Malcolm clearly does not understand, judging from the look of bewilderment on his face. I think he went along simply because I mentioned Joan.

I realize there is a lot of work ahead of us to get the welcome-home party set up and hold the attention of the adults. Putting on events like this will be good practice and help me be King of the World by age twenty.

* * *

A few days later, I have a meeting at the school library with Roberto and Maya. I want to bring them up to date on what I have learned.

"Have you guys ever heard of Robert's Rules of Order?" I begin.

They have not, so I explain. "It is how you are supposed to have a meeting."

I tell them that we had the first committee meeting the night before. "Maya's mom convened the meeting and was in charge, like the emcee," I say. Neither Roberto nor Maya is sure what *convened the meeting* means, so I get away with it. But Roberto and Maya still nod as if they understand. They are very interested in the topic.

"Did she have one of those hammer things that you hit the table with?" asks Roberto.

"Oh, a gavel," explains Maya.

I shake my head.

Maya adds, "We have a gavel in the house, though. It is cool to hit the table with it."

Maya agrees to let us test the gavel next time we are by her house.

I continue. "Anyway, Deacon Jackson emceed the meeting. She said something about calling the meeting to order, and they had an agenda that they passed around."

"The agenda is like a menu, right?" asks Roberto.

Maya jokes, "That must be why people say a meeting should come to order. The agenda is like a menu, and they're ordering from it."

We all think this is hilarious, and we laugh loudly. We are so loud we get some attention from other students, and Ms. Bridges gives us a mean look from behind her desk and signals us to be quiet.

I continue, "Then people gave boring speeches. Then Deacon Jackson read a message from Auntie Mabel saying that she wants to do some of the catering. They love Auntie Mabel and her son, but they don't like all the calories in her food."

Roberto and Maya stifle a yawn. I agree this is not the most exciting topic, and so I move on. "Anyway, Maya's mom told them about the latest diet."

This behavior was not unexpected from Deacon Jackson.

I continue my report. "Then in the middle of the meeting there was a problem. You know, uhm, whatshername from the next block—the one who calls 311 on the bodega when any of their customers make noise while walking by?"

Maya perks up. "Oh, Ms. Olive? My mom hates her. Says she's such a nuisance."

"Yeah, Ms. Olive. She is such a simpleton. In the middle of the meeting, she threatened to call 911 during the party if there are any riots. The other adults actually rolled their eyes, and no one at the meeting told them they were rude to roll their eyes."

Even though I hate Ms. Olive, I noticed she hugs me whenever she sees me, and I could swear she is often trying to hold back tears. Even though she does not say so, I know she is thinking of Joan, and I end up feeling sad also.

Right now, all three of us are aghast. "Adult behavior never ceases to amaze me," says Maya.

Roberto and I agree, and Roberto says, "If one of us kids had done that, you would never hear the end of it."

I finally get to the fun part. "Then Maya's mom said go ahead and call 911. She said Ms. Olive was off topic. Deacon Jackson cut her off while she was talking and said we were moving on to the next item on the agenda. Then Ms. Olive complained that the meeting was not following Robert's Rules of Order, and your mom really got angry and said no one in the room knew Robert's Rules of Order better than her, as she had conducted many meetings. Anyway, they argued about that for a while before they got back on topic."

Roberto is not impressed. "Why are you telling us this?"

"Well, I want to use Robert's Rules of Order for this meeting. Oh, I almost forgot—I hereby call this meeting to order." I also believe this will be good practice for when I start fixing all the things that are wrong in this world.

They both look at me like I am crazy. I ignore their rolling eyes and continue. "Anyway, the street party preparations are going according to plan. Your mom really loves this stuff, Maya—planning and organizing things. Everything is on point."

We kids agree that adults are strange and have strange ways, but we need them for certain things, as we are not allowed to do a lot of stuff.

Roberto pipes in. "So everything is ready to go?"

"Yep," I reply. "As usual, the adults have taken over the whole thing. I hate when they do that, but I guess it is a good thing. Less work for us."

Maya rubs her hands together. "This is great. I love when all I have to do is show up and look pretty."

"By the way," I add, "the committee put us on the party schedule. We have to give a speech."

Roberto and Maya groan in unison.

"I can give the speech," I say. "I will just need a little help from you guys."

The looks of agony remain on their faces. I do not let them know that I am the one on the hook for the speech as far as the welcome-home committee is concerned. Roberto and Maya will have more incentive to help me if they think they are also responsible.

CHAPTER 15

JESSE TURNED UP EARLY FOR HIS PARTY.

It was supposed to be a surprise welcome-home party for him, but he showed up a week early, hoping to surprise his mom, Auntie Mabel. Pretty soon, he found out what was going on.

No worries! Jesse apologized to everyone and even came to our committee meeting to say how bad he felt about it.

Deacon Jackson replied that it was okay. "The timeline was too close anyway. We'll push the event back a week. It will now be a general community party celebrating our youth."

"What about Joan? Maybe the party could be about Joan, too."

There is a moment of silence, then a chorus of "Yes!" and "Of course!" as everyone agrees there will be a tribute to Joan. *Any mention of Joan continues to get me attention.*

Ms. Olive wipes away a tear at the mention of Joan. It takes her a few seconds to compose herself. Suddenly, she explodes. "Deacon Jackson, you're hogging all the limelight! You've set all this up to highlight yourself instead of Jesse!"

"You are out of order!" yells back Deacon Jackson. "It was Jesse's idea to turn this into a party for the community!"

"After you pushed him out!" shouts back Ms. Olive.

I watch the adults arguing but do not take sides or say anything. Not that the adults would listen to me anyway.

Jesse glances at his watch and clearly does not want to be in the room. I do not like Ms. Olive, but in my opinion, Deacon Jackson did seem really, really, really, really, eager to allow Jesse to bow out and leave her grabbing the limelight.

So it will just be a regular street party with a tribute to Joan. No one seems to mind.

This gives everyone longer to prepare.

The whole class will attend, and Ms. Allie, Ms. Bridges, and Principal Fletcher will be there to show the school's support for the community. Ms. Bridges also says that she wants to review my speech before I give it.

The adults have taken over and will not allow us kids to have a say in the preparations. To get some control back, we kids try our hand at politics.

As Ms. Olive leaves her house for the next committee meeting, the three of us—Maya, Roberto, and I—play loudly in front of her house and make a general nuisance of ourselves.

As expected, during the next committee meeting, Ms. Olive complains about "good-for-nothing kids all over her sidewalk."

I respond, "Well, you all are not letting us take part in preparations, so we have nothing to do but play."

Because Deacon Jackson takes the side opposite Ms. Olive's in any debate, she immediately gives us some duties, thinking it will annoy Ms. Olive. Maya joins Junior, Malcolm, and their friends in designing and painting a banner to put up across the street. Roberto is given the responsibility of blowing up balloons and setting them up. He even gets some younger kids to supervise and boss around.

Deacon Jackson allows me to join her and her chief of staff as they meet with city officials to prepare the street with proper blockades and some signs. I take Roberto and Maya along. Most of the meeting is very boring, but they listen when we kids raise our hands to say something. That is nice. We feel very important and "seen."

I manage to influence them to put the main stage in front of Stinky Dump without blocking the gate. *Who says we kids don't have influence?*

Ayesha has even been lobbying me to put in a good word for her to sing the national anthem and do a dance routine with her simpleton friends.

I tell her, "No! No one wants to see your dumb dance," and she goes over my head to Deacon Jackson.

Ayesha tells Deacon Jackson that the dance will be "part of the tribute to Joan."

So now we are going to have some type of singing on the agenda along with a dumb dance routine. I consider whether I should ask Malcolm to sabotage her, but I decide that if it is for Joan, I can let it pass. Also, Malcolm would not do that. He is too nice a guy.

Anyway, I have more important things to get done than worry about Ayesha's singing and lack of dance talent.

A daring deed still needs to be done.

* * *

Two nights before the welcome party, I sneak some Krazy Glue away from my brother Junior—the same tube I saw when he and Malcolm were fixing the e-bike. I know he is not going to miss it. This is also the night when the garbage truck usually makes one of its twice-weekly visits to do some dumping. I wait until the truck arrives and the driver unlocks the metal gate and backs in. Then I sneak out of the house and quietly approach Stinky Dump.

I am worried for two reasons. One, the driver is likely to kill me if I am caught. Two, if I am caught, it will look really bad because of the fuss I made when Junior disobeyed Mom and Dad and entered Stinky Dump.

But a kid has to do what a kid has to do. I ease along the wall until I reach the corner entrance to Stinky Dump. When I reach the open gate, I peer around the corner to ensure that the driver and his assistant are behind the truck. *Ahh! Nice!* Only the driver has come this time, and he is unloading the red garbage bags by himself.

I can clearly hear the driver cursing out loud to himself. He is saying something about the developer being a cheapskate, though he does not use the word "skate." Apparently, Kaston Dagoul does not want to pay two people to do the dumping anymore, so he is saving money by having the driver do the unloading.

I approach the gate and squirt a generous amount of Krazy Glue into the lock. I make sure I do not actually go through the gate, as my parents have forbidden me from entering the lot. I do not recall them saying anything about approaching the gate, so I have not disobeyed them.

I must work quickly, because the simpleton driver is not burying the red bags this time. He is just throwing them in a pile on the ground.

I sneak back home, go to my room, and lean out the window to watch what happens next. The driver finishes up with his illegal dumping, drives the truck outside the lot, parks it, and returns to lock the gate. He lets out even more curses when he is unable to lock the gate because of the glue I applied to it. And worse for him, the gate is not properly balanced, so it keeps swinging open to block the street when he is not holding it.

The driver goes back into the lot, grabs one of the red bags, and places it outside the gate so that it keeps the gate closed. Then he takes an empty black garbage bag out of the cab of his truck and places it over the red garbage bag. It barely covers the red bag, but the driver is satisfied with this result.

I guess he thinks this is the standard of work the cheap developer is due.

This is perfect. Now in the middle of my speech, I can have Roberto and Maya remove the empty black garbage bag and reveal the red garbage bag. The gate will swing open, and the news crews, politicians, and everyone else will see the nuclear garbage inside.

It will be game over for Stinky Dump.

CHAPTER 16

WE CAN HARDLY WAIT FOR FRIDAY TO come. The three of us manage to get the day off from school to help set up the party. Ms. Allie, Ms. Bridges, and Principal Fletcher say they will come by at 7:00 p.m. Many of my classmates say they will also be coming by. I hope the simpletons do not spoil everything with their immaturity.

Malcolm, Junior, and some of their friends set up a table and a DJ booth on top of it. The DJ setup is right next to the entrance to Stinky Dump, which is right on the corner. The party will take up the rest of the street, all the way to the other corner, so the Stinky Dump entrance will be just outside the party area.

I wanted a stage to be erected, but everyone on the committee stared at me like I was crazy and said it wasn't possible. Even Todd, the newcomer from the Midwest who works as some type of social-media tech person, said it was "not logistically feasible." *And I thought these newcomers to the city were the ones who are supposed to be dreaming big things.*

Mom and Dad are really happy that I am so involved with the party. Over the past couple of weeks, they have begun to look less stressed. Junior and Ayesha have also become a little meaner. It is not full-on like before my little sister died, but I welcome it. Now I can go back to being mean to them also.

Roberto, Maya, and I have a meeting. There are two separate sheets of paper in front of us.

"Okay," I say. "This is the official speech we will show the teachers." I place my hand on one of the sheets.

"What is the difference between them?" asks Roberto.

"Only the ending," I reply. "Ms. Allie has not seen this other one, where I tell you to uncover the garbage bag blocking the gate to Stinky Dump."

I explain that the official speech has tributes where we thank the community and the adults for building a safe life for us here in Brooklyn.

Roberto warns, "Remember to be nice. You can't say anything that's annoying."

I answer, "Yep, I say in a nice way that they can ease up now and let us have our freedom now that they have created a safe world for us."

When Ms. Allie and Ms. Bridges reviewed the 'official' speech, they only had a few of what they called suggestions but we kids called corrections. Anyway, they meant well, so we agreed to the changes.

As day turned to night, a TV van from a local news station showed up. The TV van raised its antenna into the air, and that seemed to attract a crowd. Malcolm turned on the music. The food table was already set up and working.

Soon some barbecue stations turn up on the street, and food is being shared out. Spotlights make it look like daylight.

Deacon Jackson has some of her staff present, and one of them is doing the deacon's makeup and powdering her face. "If you go natural on camera," Deacon Jackson tells me, "You end up looking shiny. I get some makeup on my face so I can look correct."

I give a definite *no* when asked if I want some makeup for my speech.

After her makeup is done, Deacon Jackson takes charge of the news crew. She is going to be the first to be interviewed. They set up a nice backdrop that Deacon Jackson has provided and do several takes of an interview until Deacon Jackson is satisfied. Then the news people interview Auntie Mabel and her son. As soon as that is done, a staff member tells Deacon Jackson, the speeches will start.

By now everyone is here, and the street is crowded. My parents, brother, and sister are here. My classmates are here, along with Ms. Allie, Ms. Bridges, and Principal Fletcher. Everyone living within a few blocks of my home seems to be at the welcome-home party.

Then Malcolm cranks the music up and is playing games with his spotlights.

Suddenly I think, *I'm okay. I feel great. Never been better.* Looking around, I have not felt this happy since Joan died.

Meanwhile, I keep an eye on the entrance to Stinky Dump.

Deacon Jackson grabs the microphone from Malcolm and signals to him to stop the music. The boring speeches begin, with every politician trying to turn their five minutes into fifteen minutes. However, Deacon Jackson is very strict with the microphone, and she times everyone. She is not shy about signaling Malcolm to cut the sound and grabbing the microphone from anyone who she thinks has spoken for too long.

All activity stops for the speeches. No one can serve food. Malcolm cannot play any music. Members of Deacon Jackson's staff lurk around to be sure these rules are followed.

Finally, it is my turn to speak. I look over at my parents nervously, and they clap happily. My parents, along with Junior and Ayesha, come to the front. I hear Ayesha yelling encouragement. At first I thought she was heckling me, but she is being supportive. "Go, JR! You go, boy!"

I try to read my dad's lips, and I could swear he says to Mom, "I told you. Our son is going to be a lawyer."

I walk up to the microphone, and Deacon Jackson adjusts the stand to bring the mic down to my height. I lean in and tap the mic twice, saying, "One, two. One, two. Mic check."

Deacon Jackson covers the microphone with her hand and says to me, "There is no need for a mic check. Everything is working fine." Then she walks away. *Oh—so why do some people who are about to speak into a microphone say that?* Later, Malcolm tells me that in some arenas they do a sound check before events and say things like "Mic check."

As I am about to start my speech, I see something out of the corner of my eye. Turning the corner onto our busy street is the dump truck that makes regular illegal garbage drops at Stinky Dump.

They have chosen now to make an illegal drop.

CHAPTER 17

I START MY SPEECH WHILE LOOKING AT the truck.

I read carefully from the page in front of me. I start with the official speech. It includes some introductions that I was told to do, and it continues with "...our community has raised many brave citizens, and one of those heroes is Auntie Mabel's son, our own Jesse..."

The driver of the garbage truck hesitates upon seeing all the people present at our street fair. Normally any vehicle seeing a fair on the streets of New York would choose another route. Instead, the driver gets out and looks around. He can see that the path to the Stinky Dump corner entrance is just outside our street party and that no one is standing in front of it. He sees that he will not even have to go through the police barrier to get to the Stinky Dump entrance. He gets back into the garbage truck, puts it in gear, and proceeds slowly toward Stinky Dump.

My neighbors and those attending the street party probably assume this garbage truck has arrived early. The driver backs up to the Stinky Dump gate, gets out, and starts to walk toward the gate.

The back of the truck is beside me, about ten feet away. I stare at it, which catches the attention of the spectators closest to me, and they begin staring at the garbage truck also. The driver gets out nonchalantly and walks over to where the empty black garbage bag is being used to cover the full red garbage bag which is being used to keep the gate to Stinky Dump closed.

I quickly tell Malcolm, "Hey, shine all your lights on that truck."

The spotlight turns onto the garbage truck. Whoever wasn't already looking is definitely paying attention now. Everyone at the welcome-home party—my family and classmates, neighbors of all ages, the news team, and all the VIPs—looks at the garbage truck highlighted in the spotlight.

It is at this moment that the driver tries to pick up the garbage bag. He moves it a bit, but then he loses his grip, accidentally pulling off the black bag and dropping the red bag, which sits there, chilling, as the gate to Stinky Dump swings open.

I point and yell. "Hey, isn't that a red garbage bag? This dude is dumping nuclear garbage in our neighborhood!"

The driver stops as he hears me. He leans over the red garbage bag in front of the open gate to Stinky Dump.

Deacon Jackson runs up to me and grabs the microphone. She yells at the driver, "Hey, is there medical garbage in that red garbage bag? Are you dumping medical waste in my constituency?"

I hear the click of cameras. Cell phones are raised to take photos. The news team races over with their equipment to get the story.

Meanwhile, the driver stands, frozen and shielding his eyes from Malcolm's spotlight. He leans over the red garbage bag, so scared he is unable to move. The whole world is looking at him. I feel sorry for him, but only for a second. He is so busted.

Deacon Jackson continues to hype up the crowd, yelling into the microphone at the panic-stricken driver, "I'm talking to you! Who are you, and why are you dumping medical waste in our neighborhood under the cover of darkness?"

My dad shouts a question that is more of a comment. "Are you getting paid overtime to dump on a weekend? Time and a half? Plus a night differential?"

The driver tries to speak but can only nod. He makes the mistake of raising the red garbage bag to shield himself from the spotlight, and more pictures and videos are taken. The news team rolls into action.

I pull the microphone in Deacon Jackson's hand toward me and speak into it. "He normally comes during the week, late at night." *Wow! This is even better than me going over and pulling the black bag off the red one, the way I had planned.*

Then Auntie Mabel strides up next to me and Deacon Jackson. She shouts into the microphone, not even slowed down by the echoes and feedback as she yells, "Hey! I remember you! You were the one who grabbed JR that night when you were dumping this medical waste!"

The driver shakes in terror, trapped outside the open gate to Stinky Dump. Auntie Mabel continues. "Stay right there. You even hit JR a few times. I've been meaning to have a word with you."

Auntie Mabel releases the microphone and heads toward the shaking garbage truck driver.

However, she is cut off by my parents, who are quicker to get to the driver. "Why did you hit our son?" they shout. "Who do you think you are?"

My parents are then interrupted by my brother and sister, who jump in front of them on their way to the garbage truck driver. "Leave my little brother alone!" . . . "Wait'll I get my hands on you!" Soon, a mob is moving toward the driver.

This is great! I reach over and grab the mic again. "Yeah! Punch him! Here, hit him with this microphone! Does anybody have a baseball bat?"

I am about to suggest that the driver be put in a chokehold if no baseball bats are available, but my shouts for blood cause everyone in the crowd to stop moving forward.

My dad realizes what is happening. "No! Wait! This is just a worker trying to make some overtime."

Mom and Dad hold back the mob, including my brother and sister. The mob stops and exhales.

Part of me is sorry that cooler heads are prevailing, but I realize it is for the better.

Some cops who were working our street party walk up. The sergeant, holding a police radio, seems to be talking through his options with someone— probably a white-shirt supervisor back at the precinct.

Deacon Jackson cuts them off by speaking into the microphone. "Wait! He is not being arrested until he cleans up this mess." She turns to the driver. "Grab that shovel I see on the side of your truck that you pick up this medical waste. Take it out of here. Call that no-good developer, Kaston Dagoul, and have him send more trucks. That stuff is being moved *tonight!*"

There is a cheer from the crowd. The sergeant says something about hazmat suits being needed, but the crowd is having none of it. The police back down and appear willing to turn a blind eye to stuff being taken out immediately. "They can get hazmat suits in the morning, but get them over here tonight to start taking out the bags that are still sealed," says Deacon Jackson.

The driver picks up the shovel and walks into Stinky Dump to start removing the nuclear garbage. He mutters about not knowing the contact information for his boss. "I am just an independent contractor, a hired hand. I am not responsible for anything."

The driver starts digging, realizing that is the safest thing for him to do.

Deacon Jackson continues. "I have the developer's number. Let me call him right now. If this is not cleaned up over the weekend, then we will be in court Monday morning, and there will be serious repercussions."

I stand next to Malcolm at his DJ booth. I cannot believe that Stinky Dump is about to be cleaned up.

"Is this what you wanted?" asks Malcolm.

I nod and give him a thumbs up.

"Good job," he says.

I feel elated. I am happy to be avenging my sister's death.

A little later, more trucks appear with workers in white hazmat suits, and the cleanup is in full swing. A crowd stands around eating and keeping an eye on the cleanup.

I stand with Malcolm at the DJ booth, next to Roberto and Maya. Roberto and Maya plot how best to use the day's events to improve our status at school. I am so overjoyed at seeing all the trucks cleaning up Stinky Dump that I have not said anything.

Ms. Allie walks by me and stops to talk. "I can see why you wanted to clean up Stinky Dump. But I still don't understand why you were always so adamant about it."

I think for a moment and reply, "Because it killed my little sister. That Stinky Dump killed my little sister with nuclear garbage."

"It's really medical waste. It's not nuclear in any way."

"Whatever! It killed my little sister!" I pick up the microphone and yell into it over the music. I point into Stinky Dump at the guys in hazmat suits. "Everyone! Everyone here tonight: Those people killed my little sister!" Malcolm turns off the music.

Deacon Jackson whispers, "These are city workers trained in the handling of hazardous materials." She tries to take the microphone from me, but I keep a strong hold on it, and she gives up.

Everyone is quiet now, just listening to me. Finally, I have the attention of the adults. "They killed my little sister!" I point and shout.

I try to talk into the microphone again, but the only words that come out are "killed my little sister." Then, out of nowhere, tears fill my eyes.

Then I start to sob. Noisily! Next, Malcolm tries to take the microphone from me, but I still hold on to it. I try to stop the tears, but more tears appear. By this time I am fully crying, not knowing where all this emotion is coming from.

More tears and sobbing keep overwhelming me every time I try to speak.

"I walked her around the block to show her the neighborhood. Maybe that is when Stinky Dump poisoned her."

At the time I felt so brave as my little sister, then a toddler, grabbed my arm with both hands as we walked. She held on desperately as a semi-truck roared by and jumped with glee when I pointed out the sights of the neighborhood. She was so totally dependent on me to be her guide and protector, and I let her down.

My noisy crying continues. "Stinky Dump killed my little sister," I shout into the microphone one more time.

I finally allow Malcolm to take the microphone from me, and the only sound is of me crying. Someone leads me to a chair to sit. I continue crying. Everyone stops and looks at me, even some of the hazmat workers. I really do not care that everyone is seeing me crying, and more sobs overwhelm me. My mom hugs me, and Dad pats me gently on the shoulder. Even Junior and Ayesha have looks of concern on their faces.

Malcolm whispers softly into the microphone, "He has not cried since his little sister died, not even at her funeral. This is his time, so give him a break, okay?"

There are murmurs of understanding as people go back to what they were doing. The music is turned back on, and I continue crying.

Mom is telling someone, "Stinky Dump was always stressing him out. We always suspected there were hazardous materials there, but his little sister died from other things. Still, JR felt Stinky Dump was responsible for his sister's passing."

After a while, I lean back in my chair as my sobbing slowly subsides.

My tears eventually stop.

I suddenly feel very tired. I slowly rise and walk towards my house.

I need to get some sleep.

CHAPTER 18

I SIT ON MY STOOP ABOUT TWO weeks after the party and eat one of the currant rolls Auntie Mabel got me from the West Indian bakery, making sure to leave some for Roberto and Maya.

As I wait for them, I look over at Stinky Dump. I'll have to find a new name for it, because it is now officially cleaned up. I marvel at how quickly this was done. Why did they not just do that before?

I asked Malcolm if this was a win for us. He said, "It is hard to get a clean win in today's world. Nothing ever turns out perfectly. I don't know where they put that medical waste. Maybe they dumped it in someone else's neighborhood or put it someplace where it will mess up the environment anyway."

It made me sad that I had not gotten a clean knockout win, but that is how the real world works, I guess. Most wins are not home runs. First, you want to get on base.

At the final meeting about the street party, Deacon Jackson wanted to set up another committee on how to use the empty lot. It seems like affordable housing is something everyone wants, even Ms. Olive.

"Okay!" I tell the committee, "Stinky Dump may not have killed my sister directly, but we can still plant a tree there in her name."

In the end—this was one of the few times the adults listened to me—we agreed to plant trees all along the street. Deacon Jackson knew how to get trees from the Parks Department, and I got a promise that we would have a ceremony to dedicate one of the trees to Joan. Deacon Jackson and Ms. Olive then argued and shouted at each other over something they called "proper protocol" for getting the trees.

As I sit on the stoop, I realize things will never be the same at home without Joan. But now, whenever I think of her, I remember her unstoppable energy, along with the sound of her constant laughter, and a smile comes to my face. My family laughs during dinner whenever someone remembers one of her crazy stunts.

My dad has gone back to complaining about his children eating everything in the refrigerator. Each of the three of us blame the other two. Mom started another diet, thanks to Deacon Jackson. She asked us if we thought she needed to diet. None of us thought she did. Also, no one would join her in the diet.

My relationship with Junior and Ayesha has gone back to the way it was "back in the day." Junior told me I could not hang out with him anymore. Even Malcolm nodded in agreement. I told them they were jealous of my game as they knew I would take up the girls' attention. I generously offered to show them some moves, but instead they threw me out of Junior's basement room. They were boring anyway.

My sister Ayesha has started referring to me as Germ again and banned me from ever entering her room. This was okay as, if I get bored, I can just go back to knocking on her door until she screams. I chuckle to myself at the pleasure this gives me.

My goodwill with Ms. Allie and the other teachers has pretty much run out. They now treat me like any other kid. At least I can walk home with my friends now. *Freedom!*

Best of all, my ability to daydream properly has come back. I sit on the stoop and begin my daydreams. I have to be realistic. If anything, recent events have taught me that I will not be able to rule the world by age twenty. Maybe I can do it by age twenty-five. However, I should still be able to change it for the better—or at least a little bit—before then. *Yes, I will start by making my neighborhood better.* I'm sure there are some things I can do while I'm young and before I become an arthritic and creaky twenty-five-year-old.

I bite off a piece of currant roll and chew it while daydreaming about what I will fix.

I'm going to enjoy fixing my neighborhood.

ABOUT THE AUTHOR

R. ELLIS BROWN IS A FIRST-TIME WRITER who has lived in Brooklyn for most of his life. He uses this experience to show the positive effects that community support can have on young people.

Find out more at www.rellisbrown.com, on Instagram at r.ellis.brown, or on Bluesky at rellisbrown.bsky.social.